PUT THE KETTLE ON

TRISH TAYLOR

Put the Kettle On (Pocket Version)

by

Trish Taylor

Copyright © November 2020 by Trish Taylor

The moral right of the author has been asserted.

DISCLAIMER
This is not a travel guide and should not be your only resource when planning international travel. You should not take any of the information as serious guidance or legal advice.

www.trishtaylorauthor.com

Credits
Book Cover Design
Vanessa Mendozzi

Illustrations
Andrew Wilson

Copy Editing
Positively Proofed
info@positivelyproofed.com

ISBN: 978-1-7328655-5-6

For Jarvis

Who learned that having a British stepmom meant the answer to "What's for dinner?" was sometimes, "Shit with sugar on."

Contents

Introduction

Who is this book for?

Would you like to speak to your British friends with confidence and ease? Would you like to impress everyone with how familiar you are with the language, customs and food of the British Isles? If you plan to visit the United Kingdom, have British friends, or enjoy British TV and would like to know what the heck they are talking about, this is the book for you. *Put the Kettle On* includes information that will help you understand the language Brits use and take a peek behind the curtains of the British lifestyle.

This book has chapters on various areas of life in the UK. If you are looking for a particular word to discover its meaning, you can either:

- Go directly to the Word List, or
- Search specific items by related chapter.

(For example, words relating to cars and driving are grouped under "D" in the Word List.)

In the Word List, British words are listed first, followed by the more Americanized interpretation.

Many anglophiles are looking to find words they have heard on TV, so this approach seems easiest.

The Word List and Sayings sections offer a useful introduction to the language. It includes slang and, yes, some naughty words. Though the book mostly uses stateside spellings, there will be words and phrases that are British to help you on your journey.

Information is mostly based on my experience as a Brit who moved from the North of England to the southern United States. I have added words that may not be common but are worthy of a mention because they are funny. I have also included words that are dated, which you will find useful if you are watching classic British TV. I have avoided the inclusion of words or phrases that are offensive to specific communities. Us Brits swear. Sometimes we can be offensive and our sense of humor can be dark and edgy, although some words need to be left in the past.

Within these pages, you will find words and phrases known by most people in the UK. I am originally from Yorkshire, so there may be a Yorkshire emphasis. I haven't allocated specific chapters to regions—there are so many that doing so would only be useful to a few people.

I will indicate if a word is mainly used in the North (N), which includes Scotland and the North of England. If it's specifically Yorkshire, it will be marked with (Y). If dated, a (D).

If you think there is something missing, wrong, outdated, or you think should be added to a future edition, message me. I would love to hear from you.

Disclaimer

The information in this book is correct, as far as I am aware. Laws change, customs become outdated, and some things may be different in each of the four countries that make up the UK. Always clarify anything you are unsure of.

This book is meant to be a lighthearted and fun look at the language, customs and life in the UK. This is not a travel guide and should not be your only resource when planning international travel. You should not take any of the information as serious guidance or legal advice.

Understanding the UK and the Brits

THE UNITED KINGDOM includes Great Britain and Northern Ireland. Great Britain comprises England, Scotland and Wales. The Republic of Ireland (Irish name Éire) is not part of the United Kingdom. It is a separate country. We will mainly focus on the language, customs and habits of England and English people. I do value the customs and contributions of the other countries, but I was born and raised in England and lived there for most of my life. Most of my knowledge comes from my experience there.

The North and South of England Are Different

There is a stereotype of Northerners as being dour and miserable. In reality, you will find Northerners friendlier and chattier than our Southern cousins. Though like anywhere, if you are friendly and get to know people, you will make friends.

Accents and Regional Variations

In the UK an accent can change on average every 20 miles. Besides accents, many words differ from one region to another. The UK has counties rather than states. Each county might have a distinct accent, and the towns within the county will also have variations. Don't expect everyone to speak like the queen. The refined accent used by the upper class is known as "Received Pronunciation," or RP. It used to be that almost all presenters on TV had RP accents; regional accents were rare. There is now a more inclusive range, and you will be more surprised to hear a posh accent than a regional one. If you struggle to understand an accent while watching TV, you can put subtitles on for research. However, don't do it when you are with your Brit mates. They'll think you are a bit of a plonker.

The way Brits speak to each other can also be confusing. In various parts of the UK, you might be affectionately referred to as "Love," "Duck," "Hen," or "Cock."

Cockney Rhyming Slang

It will be useful to know some cockney rhyming slang. The rhyme comprises two words joined to make a phrase. A cockney is defined as a person born within hearing distance of the church bells of St. Mary-le-Bow, Cheapside, in the East End of London. Rhyming slang is still used in the area from which it originated and has also become more widely adopted outside of London. You also will hear it in movies and TV programs, particularly those based in London. If you hear words and phrases that are unfamiliar, keep your ears open for some of those listed below. The user will often use only part of the rhyme. For example, if you hear someone accused of telling porkies—porky pies—that means lies. Rhyming slang is said to have originated in the early

19th century by street and market traders. Rumor has it that criminals used it as code to confuse the police.

Adam and Eve: Believe. (For example, "You wouldn't Adam and Eve it.")
Apples and pears: Stairs
Aunt Joanna: Piano
Barney Rubble: Trouble
Barry White: Shite
Boat race: Face
Brown bread: Dead
Cream crackered: Knackered
Currant bun: Son
Dog and bone: Phone
Duck and dive: Hide
Gregory Peck: Neck
Loaf of bread: Head. (Ex.: "Use your loaf.")
Plates of meat: Feet
Porky pies: Lies
Rosie Lee: Tea
Septic tank: Yank
Tom tit: Shit
Whistle and flute: Suit

Brits Like Americans. Honest.

British people can differentiate the United States government from its people. They may from time to time dislike what the US is doing. They'll criticize its president or protest its foreign policy. Its people are a different matter. As long as you are behaving well, reasonable people will not hold you responsible for the actions of your country. Many Brits are straight talking and will let you know if they think you are talking bollocks. They want to like you, so let them see your best side. Visit the UK with an open mind, as most Americans do, and you will be welcomed and have a wonderful time.

The British have their own ugly Brits abroad: football hooligans and lager louts who misbehave. Just as we don't want to be associated with them, I'm sure you want to be seen as different from the occasional ugly American abroad.

No Offense

Brits can have a hard and sarcastic sense of humor. If your friend swears at you, it probably means they like you, depending on the relationship. If you are not used to it, you might not realize that what you perceive as an insult is good humored and affectionate—although it might also be because you are behaving like a wanker. Being called a name does not mean that you are being disrespected. The best way to deal with it is to allow yourself to be in on the joke. Self-deprecation is an excellent way to disarm your Brit friends.

British Problems

When not swearing or insulting you, Brits can behave in the opposite manner, being overly polite and avoiding expressing their feelings. They don't like big displays of affection. Americans are often enthusiastic and effusive with compliments. This can feel over the top to the average Brit. Because someone does not overplay compliments and emotions, it doesn't mean they don't like you. Underplay the enthusiasm, and give them time to get to know you. Everything is not considered awesome. If someone says it's OK, that is often a compliment, especially if you are dealing with Yorkshire folk.

Sorry!

Brits often say "sorry," even if an incident is not their fault. If you accidentally bump into someone at the store and they say "sorry," make sure you acknowledge them by also saying "sorry" or at the very least "no problem." Though Americans are more likely to say "excuse me" than "sorry," if you say that to a Brit, you may get the answer, "Why? What have you done?"

Tutting

If you inadvertently offend a stranger and subsequently hear a strange sound from their mouth, they may be *tutting*. A tut is a passive-aggressive way of showing disapproval. It's done by clicking the tongue on the roof of the mouth just behind the teeth. When a Brit feels offended, they may tut loudly enough to be heard, yet without acknowledging their annoyance. When the offender turns to see who tutted, the tutter can look away and feign ignorance. This could lead to an awkward interaction, which no Brit wants. If challenged with "What are you tutting about?" the tutter must decide if they will pretend it wasn't them or take it to the next level. I'm not sure what that would be—folding their arms and rolling their eyes, perhaps?

The Weather

Talking about the weather is a national pastime. It's what you do with both strangers and friends. It's often an icebreaker. Most discussions about the weather are a whinge (complaint); it's never quite right.

"Looks like we might get some rain."

"It's a bit parky."

"It's bloody freezing."

"Brass monkeys out there."

If you visit during a heat wave (warm weather lasting more than a day), it may surprise you to discover people complaining that it's too hot. Brits wait all year for the precious warm weather and forget that their homes are ill-equipped to deal with the heat. Be ready to hear:

"Blimey, it's hot."

"I'm melting."

"It's roasting."

"I'm boiling."

"It's a bit muggy." (Brits use "a bit" as a qualifier.)

Ultimately, Brits enjoy the experience of finding something they can agree on, especially how the weather is often disappointing. They are so used to complaining about it that when it brightens up and the sun eventually (albeit briefly) shines, they complain about that, too.

It doesn't rain all the time. It rains quite a lot, and there are different kinds of rain. The crucial thing to remember is that it might rain, so you need to dress appropriately and bring a brolly (umbrella). You will hear numerous descriptions for rain and raining.

Snow offers a whole other reason to complain. Although everyone gets excited about the first snowfall, they often forget that the UK is also inexplicably unable to deal with a few inches of snow. Snow will often cause major traffic issues. Even though some snow falls every year, there is collective amnesia about how to deal with it and how to drive safely without sliding into other cars.

The Shipping Forecast

Every night a comprehensive weather forecast for all the shipping areas of the United Kingdom is read aloud on BBC Radio 4. This beloved institution is a lyrical and poetic reading. Even if you do not understand what it means, it is a relaxing and meditative way to spend a few minutes and be encouraged that the world is still turning.

Bodies and Health

We have all heard the stereotype of the British and their bad teeth. The truth is Brits have teeth that are fit for purpose rather than the perfectly straight and gleaming white variety. Dental care is available, though not as easy to access under the National Health Service as is regular medical care. Anyone who wants to pay can access private dental care. In the US, it seems that people have either perfect teeth or just one in the front. In the UK, we have teeth that work, though they are not always pretty. Braces are not as common in the UK. You will rarely see an adult sporting a mouthful of iron on their gnashers. Teeth whitening is also less widespread.

The United Kingdom has a comprehensive health care system that is free at the point of service. It is funded by taxes or National Insurance Contributions and highly regarded by the majority. Criticizing it or referring to "socialized medicine" in derogatory terms will not make you popular. Though not without its faults, overall it provides incredible value for the money and wonderful service by hardworking professionals. No one in the UK needs to go bankrupt because of medical bills. People may wait for non-essential services, though a patient will never be turned away. Cancer treatments, especially for children, are some of the best available. I know people who have had fully funded, innovative and lifesaving treatment that would have left them with a lifetime of debt in the US. I do not tell you this to sway your opinion. I just want you to know that things are different in the UK and most people like it that way. If patients want to be seen quickly and have the funds, they can consult a private doctor. This allows them to jump the queue (line) and, in all likelihood, be treated by the same doctor they would see under the NHS.

Be careful with words about other's bodies. A fanny is a woman's "front bottom," so trying to buy a fanny pack could get you into trouble. No one buys fanny packs anymore, though the fashion industry will occasionally try to convince us they are back in style. If you insist you must have one, it's referred to as a "bum bag." Remember, a bum is your butt. Wearing a bum bag might identify you as an American abroad. I'd advise against it.

Education

School is for kids. Brits don't refer to college as "school." You leave school and go to college or university (uni). What Americans call the public school system is just called "school" in the UK. Public schools are fee-paying private schools. They were originally called "public" because anyone could go if they could pay. If someone says they went to public school in the UK, it means they went to a private school and paid for it.

College or university in the UK is much less focused on sports. You will not find huge-scale sports teams, and any sports scholarships are usually a contribution rather than a "full ride."

Undergraduate Degree Classification System

First Class Honors: 1st Similar to having a 4.0 GPA.
Upper second-class honors. 2:1 (pronounced two-one)
Lower second-class honors. 2:2 (pronounced two-two)
Third Class Honors: 3rd
Ordinary Degree: Not an honors degree and considered a pass only.

Work

Moaning about work nearly equals talking about the weather as a hobby for Brits. They do it in good humor. Work is to be tolerated and complained about, though if you are an employee, it is less of a stressor than in the US. Whenever an unpleasant day shows up, there is always an escape in the form of a holiday around the corner. British employees are legally entitled to paid vacations. Full-time employees get at a minimum 28 days per year. That doesn't include bank holidays, which are also usually paid. Part-timers get prorated amounts. That's why they moan about the weather; all that time off and it's bloody raining. Brits also get relatively generous maternity, paternity and adoption leave and time off for bereavement.

Employees have protection at work after two years of employment and cannot be fired without good reason. Generally, this is a good thing. Though if you have a lazy, numpty of an employee or colleague, it's hard to get rid of them as long as they stay within the rules. A worker cannot be fired for discrimination if they fall under certain protected rights.

Flags

Brits aren't particularly passionate about flags. Flags are often for cushions, royal weddings and T-shirts. The red, white and blue flag you will be familiar with is the Union Jack/Union flag—the flag of the United Kingdom. The white flag with a red cross (St. George flag) is England's national flag. Flags are sadly sometimes hijacked by racists. Since Brexit, flags have become more in vogue.

The Queen and the Royals

They are loved by many, tolerated by others and disliked, even despised, by some. The monarch has little actual power. They play a constitutional role and their power is given to parliament. Though the queen meets with the prime minister, signs off on laws and the opening of parliament, she is unlikely to use her limited power to go against what the elected government decides. You won't be sent to the Tower of London or lose your head if you speak out or insult members of the royal family. The current queen, Elizabeth II, is generally well loved. You may risk offending some of your new friends if you make fun of her, though you may also find those who are not fans of the monarchy.

The National Anthem

Brits might get emotional when they hear *God Save the Queen* at a football match. Most Brits don't care that much; it's not quite the sacred cow that it is in the United States.

Football

Our football is the game you call "soccer." The game you play with the padding and helmets? That's *American football,* which is like rugby but with the protective clothing. Brits may make fun of your footballers for being a bit namby-pamby.

Football is a passion and not a sport to be taken lightly. You might sit next to your friend at your games back home, supporting different teams and wearing opposing team shirts. That will not happen in the UK. Rivalry is serious. If you go to a game, make sure you know which team you are supporting, what end of the pitch you will sit at and what to wear.

Driving and Getting Around

IMPORTANT SAFETY NOTE. In the United Kingdom, cars are driven on the left-hand side of the road. Most of the rest of Europe drives on the right. If you take a trip across the English Channel, you will switch to driving on the right when you enter France.

A visit to the UK offers a wonderful opportunity to travel around and see the country. You could rent (hire) a car. You could also use public transport (transportation). If you decide to drive yourself, you will either need to rent an automatic or make sure you can drive a stick shift—because automatic cars are a rarity.

Being Pulled Over

If the police stop you in the UK, the patrol car will usually pull up in front of you rather than behind you. Brits are rarely armed, so a traffic stop is hopefully less of a stressful experience for all concerned, unless you are using your rental as a getaway car.

Rules on Cell Phones

Using a mobile (cell) phone while driving is prohibited. Pay heed because they strictly enforce the rules. You are not allowed to use your phone as a Satnav (GPS) unless it has a hands-free setup. It is illegal to use a hand-held phone to follow a map. The only legal use of a mobile phone is when you are safely parked, or if it is hands-free. You are *not* allowed to use your phone while stuck in traffic, at a light, or when in the passenger seat while supervising a learner (beginning) driver. The penalty is severe, especially for a new driver, who can lose their license within the first two years if found using a phone while driving.

You are expected to have your hands on the wheel. Remember that most cars are manual. (None of that driving with your knees while drinking a Slurpee.) The police have fined drivers for eating apples or chocolate bars, or for drinking coffee while driving. (Not that these acts are illegal in themselves.) If the police officer believes you were driving while distracted, they can fine you for careless driving. You must be in safe control of your vehicle. Weaving between lanes while licking a dribbling ice cream could get you an on-the-spot fine.

Drinking While Driving

Drink-driving (drunk-driving) rules are taken very seriously in the UK. It is rare to keep your license if convicted of a drink-driving offense.

No Open Container Law

Your passenger can drink as long as they are not supervising a driver. There is no law about open containers.

Driving Age

People start driving at 17, although there are exceptions for driving on private land.

Speed Cameras

Closed-circuit cameras are everywhere in the UK, as well as speed cameras. You usually get plenty of notice with warning signs, though you may not realize that you have driven past a camera because not all of them flash. Unlike a police officer, who might be lenient, if you are only a few miles over the speed limit, a speed camera has no such flexibility. Some cameras are set with a threshold by individual police forces (believed to be around 10%). There is no guarantee, and some police forces refuse to confirm or deny that they have a threshold at all. Some poor buggers have been fined for going just a few miles over the limit.

Smaller Cars

Although the British like cars and driving, they don't all feel the need to drive enormous ones, sometimes known as a "big fuck off car." Many cars on the road are small compared to US models. When you encounter single-track roads in villages and smaller towns that need careful maneuvering, you will be grateful if you rented a more modest car.

Traffic Lights

As far as I know, there is no "right turn on red" allowed anywhere in the UK. (Although, technically, it would be a turn to the left since Brits drive on the left side of the road.) When you are at a busy intersection trying to turn left, someone will let you out if you are lucky. Remember to do the same for someone else next time. Lights do not turn from red to green as they do in the US. There is always an amber (orange) light in-between red and green.

There is no rule regarding stopping for school buses or funerals (as in the US). For the most part, there is little need to worry about school buses anyway. Most school kids get on regular public transport, are driven by their parents, or walk.

Directions

If you ask for directions, especially if a roundabout is involved, you will be told to take a numbered exit or to go left or right. People rarely say, "go east or west," unless they are talking about westbound or eastbound on a motorway.

White Van Man

This is a stereotype referring to the driver of a "transit van," which is a small works vehicle driven by a tradesperson. They often exhibit aggressive driving and behave in a selfish and antisocial manner. A white van man is seen as an insult.

Buses

A wide variety of the public uses buses, which run late into the night in cities and are a primary way of getting around. Bus services offer special rates for Old Age Pensioners (OAPs) to encourage them to use the bus at "off-peak" times. You would say *getting the bus* rather than *riding the bus*.

Trains

Train travel can be very expensive in the UK. If you want to travel by train, you will find booking ahead can save you a lot of money. A ticket booked a few weeks or months in advance can cost a fraction of the price of one bought closer to departure time. Trains booked in advance may not be transferable and are specific to one seat, train and train line (company). Trains are comfortable, with a buffet car for refreshments and often WiFi.

Strikes/Industrial Action

Public transport strikes are not uncommon. If you are planning a trip on a train or will use the subway in London, check for updates regarding potential industrial action or strikes.

Weekend Maintenance

You may also find that trains are unavailable on weekends because of scheduled maintenance. This is often specific to London. They offer a replacement bus service if the train you need is not running. Always plan ahead, give yourself plenty of time and expect the unexpected.

Look Right, Look Left, Look Right Again

When walking in towns and cities near roads, please remember that the traffic is coming from the opposite direction of what you are used to. Because cars drive on the left side of the road, you must get used to looking right (instead of left) before you step out into traffic.

The Highway Code

Offers official information on the rules of the road in the UK. Check it out: www.gov.uk/guidance/the-highway-code

For words and phrases about cars and driving, look under "D" in the Word List.

Food and Shopping

WE BEGIN another chapter with a stereotype, this time about bad English food. One theory is that it came from US servicemen who were in the UK during World War II. Of course, the food wasn't great because of rationing related to the war. If you look for crappy food, you can find it. You can also find fabulous food. Buy a guidebook, look on TripAdvisor or any online guide. Do not let ignorance and laziness stop you from enjoying some wonderful food, often at a very reasonable price.

Class and Meals

How you refer to your meal in the UK may say something about your perceived class:

Working Class or Northern
Dinner: Middle of the day.
Tea: Evening meal.
Supper: A snack before bed.

Middle Class
Lunch: Middle of the day.
Dinner or supper: Evening meal.

High Tea

High tea or afternoon tea isn't the big thing that Americans often think it is. An overpriced high tea at an expensive hotel is mainly a tourist activity or a birthday treat. A small cafe serving cakes and hot drinks or a cream tea with scones, jam and clotted cream is a much better alternative if you want substance over style. (See the Homes, Telly and Tea section.)

Though you can identify items from sight while shopping, you may find it helpful to know local names for these items, especially when buying fresh produce and using self-checkout. See the Food Directory below for a list of common British food names and more useful information.

Fresh items are sold by the kilogram and not by the pound, though you may find some stores still unofficially using the old system. (See the Metric and Measurements section under "M" in the Word List.)

Food Traditions and Popular Meals

(NOTE: When baking, Brits use kitchen "weighing scales" rather than cups for measuring ingredients.)

The Chippy: The fish-and-chip shop

Fish and chips: A piece of cod or haddock coated in batter and deep-fried, accompanied by chips (fries). Traditional fish-and-chip shops fry using beef dripping. Vegetable oil is used in many places.

Accompaniments include:
Mushy peas
Curry sauce
Salt and malt vinegar

Fishcake: A potato-and-fish patty coated in batter and fried.

Buttered teacake: A large, soft, buttered bread roll.

Chip butty: Chips in a buttered teacake. (N)

Fish butty: A portion of fish in a buttered teacake. (N)

Battered sausage: A large sausage link coated in batter and fried.

The Carvery

A carvery is often found in a restaurant attached to a pub or hotel. This dining experience is like an American buffet and features various roasted meats. This is a very British institution and another way for Brits to eat their favorite roast dinner. The diner chooses their meat, which is then "carved" for them as they line up with their plate. The meal includes an array of side dishes and traditional puddings/desserts.

Seaside Food

The British seaside has its own food delights. Expect to find seafood, including cockles, mussels, crabs, winkles and whelks. You will also find food similar to that from an outdoor funfair (similar to a county or state fair in the US).

A 99

A proper ice cream van (truck) that sells soft-serve ice cream will also sell a 99, which is a cone of soft ice cream with a Cadbury's chocolate flake inserted and topped with raspberry sauce. Delicious, or as we might say, bloody gorgeous! Other additions include chopped nuts or "hundreds and thousands." That means sprinkles!

A Stick of Rock

This is a delightfully British confection usually only found at the seaside. A stick of rock—sometimes shortened to "rock"—is a hard, cylindrical candy stick, usually with the name of the town or resort printed through it. They are often peppermint flavored, sometimes aniseed, though there are many varieties, styles and sizes available.

The Sandwich Shop/Bakers

Traditional bakers selling sandwiches using their own baked bread are not as easy to find as they once were. Nowadays, they have been mostly replaced by high-street (main-street) chains. They offer good variety and value for the money. Chocolate eclairs, apple cream donuts, cream horns, custard slices, millionaire's shortbread, sausage rolls and savory "pasties" are just some of the yummy stuff you can find in shops on almost every high street.

Bread

The name given to bread rolls can be confusing. Depending on where you live or your background, what you call your bread could be any of the following (and probably some I have never heard of).

Brits can make a sandwich out of anything. The fish finger sandwich (fish sticks) has now become gentrified as a popular pub meal. If you've never had a crisp sandwich, you've probably never run out of food or been a poor student.

Cakes and Desserts

(Also called puddings, afters or sweets.)

Look out for some of these favorites.

Apple crumble
Arctic roll
Eton mess
Jam roly poly
Lemon drizzle cake
Parkin
Pavlova
Rice pudding
Spotted dick
Sticky toffee pudding
Sherry trifle
Victoria sandwich cake

Full English Breakfast

A full English is a splendid way to start the day. (Also known as a "fry-up.") Served in pubs and cafes, you can usually find vegetarian options of the meat products.

Expect to find some or all of these: bacon, sausage, mushrooms, fried bread, tinned (canned) tomatoes, baked beans, black pudding (N), toast and tea or coffee.

Coffee

Many Brits drink instant coffee. It's widely available with lots of options. If you go to a pub or cafe, specify if you want freshly brewed coffee.

Pizza

Brits do pizza differently. Some toppings that you might find weird are not only normal but positively compulsory. After getting over the shock of putting beans on our toast, you will have to accept that we put fish on our pizzas.

Pizza Toppings

Tuna and sweetcorn
Prawn
Ham and pineapple
Seafood pizza. (May include prawn and tuna.)
Bolognese pizza. (Topped with Bolognese sauce.)
Keema pizza. (In areas of the UK where pizzas are sold in Indian takeaways (to-go), you might also have curry on top of your pizza.)

A Word About Chocolate

Many Brits don't enjoy American chocolate. We are not trying to be rude when we say it tastes like vomit, or that it has a weird aftertaste. A necessary additive in some US chocolate—added to stop chocolate from melting in warmer climates—causes an aftertaste that Americans don't usually notice. Without this additive, British chocolate melts more quickly. Some Americans find that British chocolate tastes weird to them, too.

Easter Eggs

Visit the UK before Easter and you will find a massive selection of chocolate Easter eggs. Most chocolate and sweets manufacturers make their own version, usually with one of their products inside a hollow chocolate egg or in a box. You can find vegan, gluten-free, white chocolate, milk, dark, luxury, children's, fair-trade and eggs with the recipient's name or message written on it in chocolate icing. It is a joy to behold, and once you have experienced a proper Easter egg, you will no longer consider a plastic one a suitable alternative—unless you hate chocolate or have no soul.

Shopping

When Brits refer to "going shopping," it means any kind of shopping. They rarely differentiate between grocery shopping and any other kind.

You will need a "bag for life," a reusable shopping bag. Those bags you always forget and leave in the car are a necessity in the UK. Stores do not give away plastic grocery bags for free. Retailers are legally obligated to charge you for any bags they give you, with few exceptions. Equally, bagging your fruit and veggies in single-use plastic bags is not recommended if you don't want to be judged. Take your own bag; you are helping save the planet.

For the commitment phobes out there, you don't have to keep your bag for life forever. You can switch it up and choose from a range of beautiful bags. They are "for life" only because if they ever break, you get them replaced for free—if you remember to take them out of your car. To some shoppers' horror, you won't be automatically given a bag, even if you buy a beautiful item of clothing. That is, unless you pay for it or if the store provides their own paper bags.

Trolley (Shopping Cart)

Because people steal and dump trolleys (shopping carts), supermarkets installed a mechanism that required the insertion of a pound coin to release the trolley for use. When the cart is hooked back into place via a chain, your coin is returned. It's always worth having a pound coin just in case you need it. You can also buy key rings with a pound-coin-shaped token. (This changed post-COVID and is subject to revert back at any time.)

The UK does not charge additional sales tax. The price you see is what you pay, though it may include Value Added Tax (VAT) on applicable items.

Money

The United Kingdom uses the pound rather than the Euro, which is used in much of Europe. Scotland has its own pounds, which you may find you cannot use in an English shop. There are decades of debate around whether Scottish money is legal tender. All my research shows that by the technical definition of what legal tender means, Scottish money is not legal tender, even in Scotland. If you visit Scotland and are given change, know that you could have trouble spending it in other parts of the UK. Personally, I have never had a store refuse it, and I have worked in retail stores that have been happy to take it.

The Republic of Ireland uses the Euro.

Food List

FOODS, including their American Counterpart or Alternative

Angel Delight: Instant pudding

Aubergine: Eggplant

Black Treacle: Similar to molasses. (Rich, dark treacle used in toffee and some rich cakes like gingerbread.)

Boiled sweets: Hard candy

Branston Pickle: Brown pickle. (Comes in jars with chopped vegetables.)

Brown sauce: Steak sauce. (Thicker in consistency.)

Biscuits: Cookies

We must explore biscuits a little further because they are an important part of British education. British biscuits are less chewy and more crunchy.

Digestive biscuits: Similar to graham crackers. (Also see chocolate digestives, even better.)

Rich tea biscuits: Simple biscuit (An excellent accompaniment to tea).

There is a vast array of toffee-, cream- and chocolate-filled delights in the biscuit aisle of the supermarket.

Jaffa Cakes: The orangey, chocolaty deliciousness that are Jaffa Cakes has created serious debate on whether it is a biscuit or a cake. Though you will find it in the biscuit aisle, they are officially defined as a cake. The decision became a legal one as cakes and biscuits are taxed differently. Whatever it is, you owe it to yourself to try one, whether you eat the layer of chocolate first, peel off the orange with your teeth or bite into the entire thing, it's up to you.

Beans on toast: Toasted and buttered bread, topped with baked beans, sprinkled with a little pepper and maybe some cheese on top. Delish! (Not as weird as it sounds.)

Beetroot: Beets

Black pudding: Savory pudding made of blood. (This *is* as weird as you think.)

Broad beans: Fava beans

Candy floss: Cotton candy

Caster sugar: Refined sugar. (Used in baking.)

Cheese on toast: Grilled cheese

Cheese toastie: Panini

Chicory: Endive

Chips: French fries

Coriander: Cilantro

Corn on the cob: Corn

Corn flour: Cornstarch

Courgette: Zucchini

Cream tea: Scones with jam and cream—clotted cream is preferable—and a pot of tea.

Served in cafes, more traditionally in Cornwall and Devon, but also available elsewhere.

Crisps: Chips

Crumpets: A breakfast treat similar to an English muffin, yet softer, fluffier and more delicious. Served with butter. (Available in the bread aisle at the supermarket.)

Curry: The UK has adopted Indian curry as the unofficial national dish. (See Pubs and Restaurants section.)

Custard: A sweet sauce poured over puddings to create the perfect comfort food.

Dripping: Rendered animal fat (grease) produced during cooking. This leftover product, once spread on bread and eaten out of necessity because of poverty, has seen a popular resurgence as diet trends have changed.

Double cream: Heavy cream

Eggs with soldiers: Soft-boiled eggs with sliced strips of bread or toast (soldiers). If you like runny eggs and comfort food, this is for you. You will need eggcups.

Eggy bread: French toast

Faggots: Meatballs

Fairy cakes: Cupcakes

Fish fingers: Fish sticks

Flan: Fruit pie

Gammon: Salted and cured ham similar to Virginia ham.

Gherkin: Pickle

Golden Syrup: A rich treacle; the secret ingredient to many cake and biscuit recipes.

Ice pop: Popsicle

Icing: Frosting

Icing sugar: Powdered sugar

Knickerbocker glory: Ice cream sundae. (Outdated, but what a fabulous name.)

Jacket potato: Baked potato

Jam: Jelly

Malt loaf: A rich, dense and fruity bread (with consistency of cake and often eaten with a spread of butter).

Marmite: A love-it-or-hate-it spread made of yeast extract. (A little goes a long way. Try it on toast.)

Marrow: Squash

Minced meat/mince: Ground beef. (Not to be confused with mincemeat, a sweetened, dried fruit mixture eaten in pies at Christmas.)

Piccalilli: Mustard-based pickle/relish of spiced, chopped vegetables.

Pickled eggs: Boiled eggs pickled in seasoned vinegar or brine. (See Pub section.)

Pickled onions: Bite-size onions pickled in vinegar.

Pies: When Brits refer to pies, they almost always mean the savoury (savory) variety.

Pigs in blankets: Small chipolata sausages wrapped in bacon. (Popular at Christmas.)

Pips: Seeds

Plain flour: All-purpose flour

Pop: Soda. (Traditional flavors include cream soda and dandelion and burdock.)

Porridge: Oatmeal

Prawn cocktail: Small shrimp in a "Marie Rose" cocktail sauce. (British cocktail sauce is similar to Thousand Island dressing. A pale pink-colored mixture of tomato ketchup and mayonnaise with spices.)

Prawn: Shrimp

Rocket: Arugula

Salad cream: A very British condiment. (More frequently used in sandwiches than salads; tastes like mayonnaise with the consistency of ranch dressing.)

Scones: Similar to American biscuits but sweeter. (Sometimes with sultanas served with jam and cream or butter.)

Single cream: Pouring cream. (The closest alternative would be half and half.)

Smarties: Sugar-coated chocolate candies. (Different from the US candy, more like M&Ms, a shell filled with chocolate.)

Spring onions: Green onions/scallions

Squash/cordial: Sweet fruit concentrate. (Made to be diluted with water; a children's drink or a mixer with alcohol.)

Sultanas: Golden raisins

Swede: Rutabaga

Toad in the hole: Sausages baked into Yorkshire pudding

Toffee apple: Candy apple

Water biscuits: Crackers. (The type you put cheese on. Please don't dunk these in your tea.)

Wholemeal: Whole wheat

Worcestershire sauce: Spicy sauce. (Used in cooking and a splash in a Bloody Mary. Pronounced as two syllables: wuster.)

Yorkshire pudding: A savory accompaniment to a roast dinner. (See Pub section.)

Pubs, Restaurants and Drinking Culture

WATCH a British soap opera and you might believe that most Brits spend every night in their local (the pub). Although pubs are still popular, the availability of inexpensive alcohol from supermarkets has contributed to many pubs closing their doors. In many towns, the local pub has been replaced by chain pubs offering cheap drinks and even cheaper food. You can still find excellent food and warm hospitality in pubs, especially in destination and country pubs.

Brits love to drink. If you don't drink, they may treat you with suspicion. There is a view that if you are the sober one, you may take note of other's inappropriate behavior.

The legal drinking age in the UK is 18. As a visitor, you are allowed to drink at 18 even though the drinking age in the US is 21. It is not unusual for young people to be given alcohol at home. The law says you can't give alcohol to children under five. Above that age, it's the parents' decision. Children are also allowed in pubs with beer gardens and allowed in at 16 if accompanied by an adult and not consuming alcohol. (Although this is at the bar owner's discretion.) Overall, the attitude toward drinking in the UK is fairly relaxed.

There are many names for being drunk. The only one that I have never heard anyone say in the UK that is popular in the US is "sloppy drunk." For many Brits, the whole idea of getting drunk is to reach the point of sloppiness! Here are some that may be new to you.

Remember, there are CCTV cameras everywhere, so being drunk in public (though actively encouraged by your friends) may have you starring in a reality TV show. Seeing yourself vomiting your curry into the gutter or having sex up against a skip (dumpster) is not how you want to be remembered.

Types of Pubs

The local: Often a small, simple pub where everyone knows each other. (These are dying out as more people drink at home.)

Chain pubs: Inexpensive drinks and food.

Gastro pubs: Upmarket (more upscale) dining.

Country pubs: Usually in scenic spots with seating outside and an excellent selection of food and beer.

Micropubs: Small, independent establishments offering craft beers.

Pub Food

Traditional pub food has come a long way from the pie and a pint, including:

Pickled Eggs

If you think this is a weird concept, you are not alone. You may see this unusual delight sitting on the bar in the local pub—boiled eggs, swimming in a huge jar, reminiscent of a mad scientist's medical specimen, but pickled in vinegar or brine rather than formaldehyde. Many Brits have never eaten one, either. Don't ask too many questions about how long it has been sitting there, though they can last for months. Honestly.

Ploughman's (Plowman's) Lunch

Although a "Ploughman's" was originally a simple meal that the ploughman could take into the field and eat cold between ploughing, it has evolved into a much fancier affair at some pubs. A Ploughman's usually is a combination of thick, crusty bread, a hunk of cheese, often with ham, or a slice of meat pie, an apple and assorted pickles. This is not the spear of pickle (a gherkin) you are used to, but a smeary, brown, crunchy concoction that looks strange but tastes surprisingly good. Like most things new to your palate, it might be an acquired taste.

Crusty Sandwiches/Baguettes

Brits are big fans of sandwiches or "sarnies." And there's nothing better than a doorstep sandwich: big, thick hunks of bread with your choice of filling or maybe a filled French baguette or crusty bread.

Yorkshire Pudding

Although Yorkshire pudding is usually a small, shallow, oven-fried pancake mixture eaten with a roast dinner, pubs often sell filled Yorkshire puddings. A "Yorkie" the size of your plate will be filled with savory gravy and possibly meat and vegetables. Never confuse British gravy for the American kind. Gravy is brown.

Pie and Peas

A hot meat pie with fillings that could include steak and kidney, pork or a vegetarian option. Green peas are "steeped" overnight with water and bicarbonate of soda (baking soda), then boiled to make a mushy paste. Mushy peas are another misunderstood food item. They sound disgusting yet are surprisingly good with pies and especially with the obligatory mint sauce.

Sunday Roast

A beloved meal in the UK is the Sunday dinner or Sunday roast, served both in the home and in pubs and restaurants. A traditional roast includes meat, which is often roast beef, roast potatoes and Yorkshire puddings. If you're lucky, lunch may be followed by a traditional sweet pudding.

Other Pub Menu Items

Bangers and mash: Sausage and mashed potato.

Beef hotpot: A stew topped with sliced potatoes.

Fat chips: Exactly what they sound like.

Fish and chips: Fish and French fries.

Ham, egg and chips: Simple but good.

Jacket potato: Baked potato. (Often served with a choice of fillings.)

Scampi and chips: Fried shrimp in breadcrumbs.

Scotch egg: Boiled egg wrapped in sausage meat and coated in breadcrumbs.

Shepherd's pie: A savory mashed-potato-topped pie with a ground meat base. (Traditionally, Shepherd's pie uses lamb. If a different meat is used, it is considered a cottage pie.)

Toad in the hole: Sausages cooked in Yorkshire pudding.

Welsh rarebit: Fancy toasted cheese. (Often cooked in beer.)

Puddings

Sticky toffee pudding: A rich pudding made with dates.

Apple crumble: Cooked apples covered with a crumbly unconstructed pastry.

Banoffee pie: Banana and toffee cheesecake.

Pavlova: Fruit- and cream-topped meringue pie.

Treacle tart: Pastry filled with sweet and sticky treacle.

Sherry trifle: Layers of Jelly (Jell-O), laced with sherry, custard, fruit and cream.

Getting a Round In

When drinking in a group, it is customary to take turns ordering and paying for drinks. This is known as "getting a round in." If you are in a small group, it's simple to navigate. After someone has bought a round, the next person volunteers. If there is a sizable group, it can be awkward and expensive. There may be times when someone will pronounce, "I'll get these in," without the expectation that the rounds will continue. If you don't want to get into a round because of cost or maybe you are only drinking soft drinks, you can declare. "I will get my own. I'm only having one. I'm driving," or whatever reason you don't want to be in the round. Whatever you do, don't join a round and then not "pay your way." You will be known as a tight arse or someone who never puts their hand in their pocket. Going to the loo just as the drinks are about to be ordered is an obvious ruse you will not get away with. As the visiting American, they may well buy into the stereotype that you have a lot of money. If you do have deep pockets, feel free to say, "The drinks are on me," or if you're feeling flush, "Drinks all round." Be careful. This could cost you more than your flight home.

If you are in the pub with friends, someone will usually get the crisps in. Crisps are a big part of the pub tradition. Don't buy a bag and sit and eat them by yourself. The Brits who got the round in will often also buy a selection of crisps. The bags are then put on the table and split open so everyone can share.

Working Men's Clubs

Although less popular than they once were, working men's clubs are still an institution in some parts of the North of England. Although open to anyone, they were established for working men. Until fairly recently, women were banned from going to the bar or sitting in men-only rooms in some clubs. Clubs have entertainment, bingo, cheap drinks and often a raffle where you may go home with the raw ingredients for your Sunday roast or cooked breakfast.

Drinks

Many of the drinks you are familiar with are available in UK pubs and bars. There may be some that are new to you or that have different names.

Bitter: Dark beer. (Once the most popular drink in a pub; has been overtaken by lager.)

Gin and tonic: A G&T was once the only way to drink gin. You can now find gin of every flavor. (Gin bars are a huge trend, serving a wide range of craft gins flavored with herbs, spices and exotic additives.)

Ginger wine: Fortified ginger drink, sipped with or without ice or added to Scotch whisky to make a whisky mac.

Ice and a slice: If your bartender inquires if you would like ice and a slice, they are offering ice and a slice of fresh lemon. (Remember, ice is a cube or two. Don't expect to be given half a glass full.)

Lager: Light-colored or blonde beer, also served with lime. (Ask for lager and lime, or lager and black —black currant juice—which is also popular. People also drink cider and black. Cider is always alcoholic. There is no sweet, fruity, non-alcoholic cider. That's just called apple juice.)

Lemonade: A clear, fizzy soda-type drink similar to 7-UP. (What Americans call lemonade is called "cloudy" or "traditional" lemonade.) Lemonade is used as a mixer with beer and shots, as well as served to children.

Lime and soda: A shot of sweet lime juice topped up with on-tap soda water. (This is an inexpensive and refreshing choice if you are driving or not drinking alcohol. Popular because it's cheap.)

Shandy: Lemonade mixed with beer. (The perfect gateway drink to a lifetime of alcohol abuse.)

Shandy top: A splash of lemonade in your beer.

Stout: Strong dark beer.

Short: Liquor. (If someone offers to buy you a short with your drink, that's a shot of liquor or something from the optics, also known as a chaser.)

Snakebite: Half lager and half cider in a pint glass. (Drink with extreme caution. Something about the chemistry of these drinks in the same glass has the potential to cause the imbiber to become an arsehole.)

Snowball: A mixture of Advocaat (an alcoholic eggnog), lemonade and a splash of lime juice. Mixed to make it frothy. (This old-fashioned drink is popular with elderly aunts. Don't expect all bar staff to know how to make it.)

Sweet Sherry: Fortified wine. (Another one popular with mature ladies.)

A Swift Half

If you're invited to go to the pub for a swift half or a cheeky half, that is a ruse to get you to the pub. (Once there, you will be unlikely to leave after said half.)

Water

You may have to ask for water. If you are eating in a pub, water is not always brought to the table. If you want water, be sure to clarify that you want tap water or they may serve you mineral water, which comes at a cost.

Soda

If you are having a soft drink or soda with your meal, remember that refills are rarely offered. Also, you may have to ask for ice.

Last Orders

Licensing laws have changed over the past two decades, and "last orders" is not what it was. Traditionally near closing time, the publican (pub owner) would call "last orders," which was your last chance to get a drink. At closing time, they called "time." After that, you were in "drinking-up time," a window of time to finish your drink.

Nowadays, pubs don't have the same strict rules and can serve drinks within their license whenever they want. A landlord or landlady of the pub can still tell you to "drink up" when they've decided it's time to close. Make sure you know the closing time so you don't have to rush that last pint.

Food Orders and Shared Tables

When eating in pubs, you almost always order at the bar. When ready, the food is brought to your table. Although some will have a dining area where you may book a table, others will serve your bar-ordered food at the regular tables where others are drinking. If the place is busy, you may not get a table to yourself. Although customary to ask if it's OK to share a stranger's table, it is not unusual to do so, and most people will not refuse. In a cafe or casual dining restaurant in the US, you will be less likely to share a table with a stranger. In the UK, if there is a table for four with only two people sitting, they will not shun you for asking to sit with them, even if it feels a little awkward. Better to feel awkward than try to balance your pie and peas with your pint of lager.

Drinking outside is allowed, and if the sun is shining, it's virtually compulsory.

Restaurants

British people use a knife and a fork. That's why they put both on the table in the restaurant. If you insist on using your fork to cut your food, you will not pass the Brit test. You might be sent to the children's table until you learn to eat properly.

Curry and Indian Food

While in the UK, make sure to experience food from Indian, Pakistani or Bengali restaurants, or any international eatery, which are the byproduct of international visitors and migrants over the last few decades. You will be spoiled by the abundance of takeaway and restaurant choices.

Tipping

Tipping is not an expectation. All employees are paid at least the minimum wage. The customer is not expected to make up their wages in tips. If you have a good meal, a tip upwards of 10% will be appreciated. Brits don't normally tip bar staff. It is customary to say "and whatever you are having" or "have one for yourself." The bar person may then agree to "have one later" and take the amount equal to a drink and put it in their tip jar.

The Cinema (Movies)

The cinema has similarities and some marked differences to US movie theaters. It might surprise or even disgust you to discover that Brits often prefer to eat their popcorn sweet. It was once the only kind available. Now you can also get salted popcorn. Ice cream is also served at the cinema, and some theaters have bars with wine and beer.

Invitations

If you are invited to a celebration or an event, Brits expect you to attend as agreed and to be on time. Brits in the US are often surprised to discover that a plan may not be a firm commitment. They expect a commitment to their invite, and it may be more formal. Brits often dress up even when they attend an event at someone's home. Check what they expect of you before you accept an invitation. If your host has arranged a sit-down dinner, they will be pissed if you show up when they are serving dessert.

If the invite says 7 for 7:30, that indicates that you are welcome to come any time after 7 p.m. and will sit to eat at 7:30 p.m. Dinners in the US are often earlier than in the UK. The only time most Brits would eat at 6 p.m. would be if they were trying to get an early bird special (usually offered to OAPs), a two-for-one deal, or eating with children. Eating at 6 p.m. is old people dinnertime.

Holidays, Celebrations, Gardens and Outdoors

A HOLIDAY IS A VACATION. Most people in the UK go on holiday at least once a year and also go on day trips and weekends away on bank holidays—what you call Federal holidays. Travel within Europe is relatively inexpensive and convenient. You can be in France in a couple of hours if traveling from the South of England. Some people go just for shopping or to buy wine, known as a "booze cruise."

Bonfire Night or Plot Night

On Nov. 5, the country comes together to celebrate Guy Fawkes's failed 17th-century plot (the Gunpowder Plot of 1605) to blow up the Houses of Parliament. They burn his effigy on bonfires and set off fireworks. More recently it has become popular to burn effigies of political leaders or celebrities who have fallen out of favor.

Pancake Day/Shrove Tuesday

On Pancake Tuesday, or the British version of Mardi Gras, we drag out the frying pan and try to remember how to make pancakes. British pancakes are similar to French crepes. A small amount of batter is drizzled into a pan of hot oil. Perfect pancakes are flipped halfway through the cooking process. They're traditionally served sprinkled with lemon juice and sugar, rolled and eaten immediately.

Barbecues (BBQ)

If you're invited to a bank holiday barbecue, expect to be outside whatever the weather. Even if it's freezing, you will still be outside and surrounded by Brits wearing sundresses and shorts. Don't expect a rack of ribs. You are more likely to be offered a burnt sausage.

Christmas and Boxing Day

Christmas in the UK extends into the day after Christmas. Boxing Day is a bank holiday, which means most workers have a paid day off. It is thought to originate from times when servants were required to work on Christmas Day. They were given the day after Christmas off and would be given a gift—a Christmas box. It also became common to give tradespeople such as window cleaners and milkmen a Christmas box, though not necessarily on Boxing Day. Think of it as a B-list Christmas. It's a day to lounge around, play with the stuff you got for Christmas, eat leftovers and sometimes play party games with the people you didn't get to see the day before.

Christmas Cards

It is common to give Christmas cards to friends and work colleagues. Brits also say Happy Christmas more commonly than Merry Christmas. It's a habit, possibly from the idea that "Merry" was linked to drunkenness.

Christmas Crackers

This popular table decoration includes a party hat, a toy and a corny joke or riddle. Almost every home has crackers at Christmas. They make a crack sound when pulled. The person who ends up holding the biggest piece wins the enclosed gift or toy. Crackers range from cheap and cheerful with a plastic novelty to luxurious options that include expensive watches and trinkets. You can also make your own or buy pre-cut kits.

A word of caution: Don't try to ship or bring crackers into the US. The mechanism that causes the crack uses a tiny amount of gunpowder. Importing explosives is illegal. You can find crackers in some stores in the US. They are sometimes known as "poppers." A cracker is not an offensive term in Britain. Asking for poppers, however, could get you into a different type of trouble.

Wetting the Baby's Head

In the past, this referred to a father's celebratory drink with friends while the mother recovered after delivering her baby. Nowadays it can include any celebration of the birth of a baby.

Gardens and Outdoors

Brits love their gardens and gardening. On weekends, you will find crowds at the garden center buying plants and garden equipment. A yard is an appropriate word for a paved area; a garden is where you grow stuff.

Walking

The United Kingdom has wonderful places to walk. Yes, it might rain, but it won't last forever. According to famous British fellwalker and guidebook author Alfred Wainwright, "There is no such thing as bad weather, only unsuitable clothes." A fellwalker is someone who hikes over fells (hills/mountains).

There are no alligators, poisonous snakes or spiders, and it's rare for anything to bite or eat you. We don't have hurricanes. (OK, well there was that one that once took everyone by surprise.) There are four distinct seasons, even if they all have some rain.

Watch the weather forecast, talk to people about the weather, and if it rains, you can always go to the pub. The UK has lots of places where you can walk. You will find pavement and footpaths everywhere.

The National Trust

If you want to explore Britain's history and culture and support a charitable cause, visit a National Trust property. The Trust is a conservation charity. It takes care of and protects many historic buildings, collections and gardens and, yes, it has castles. We know that Americans like castles! The Trust also cares for miles of coastline, woodlands and countryside. You can become a member or visit just one property during your trip. You will find knowledgeable volunteers who will share the history of the property. There are often tearooms where you can enjoy delicious food in a beautiful setting and sometimes a gift shop to buy original souvenirs. This is a marvelous way to enjoy the countryside.

The Tip/Recycling Center

When Brits want to get rid of their junk, they take a trip to the "Tip." This is similar to a landfill or dump, but it's where individual homeowners take their excess rubbish rather than where the rubbish trucks go. The Tip also takes recycling and hazardous waste, such as used oil or batteries. On busy bank holidays, there is often a line of cars waiting to offload their waste from a weekend of Do It Yourself (DIY). If the Tip is closed or busy, some people illegally dump their waste elsewhere. This is known as fly-tipping.

Homes, Telly and Tea

THE AVERAGE BRITISH home is smaller than those in the US, often with compact rooms and less likely to be an open plan. Many homes are old but built to last. They are also often closer to each other, unless you are fortunate enough to live in the country or in a large house.

The Letterbox

British homes have a letterbox in the front door through which the postman makes his delivery. The familiar sound of the letterbox opening and the plop of post on the mat brings great joy, especially if it is your birthday, less so if you are avoiding debt collectors. If you live in a less desirable area or you have pissed off your neighbors, you might want to seal it up around Bonfire Night. A firework through your letterbox is not a good way to celebrate our most famous terrorist. If you want to post a letter, you will have to find a post box. The postman does not collect mail; he only delivers it.

Windows

Windows don't have screens because there aren't that many bugs. People often open their windows for fresh air. Most British homes do not have air conditioning.

Window Cleaners

Window cleaners are still popular in the UK. This is a self-employed tradesperson who comes around with their ladder and a bucket to wash your windows. (I hear they have become fancy and now often use telescopic window cleaners.) You usually contract them to wash your windows every fortnight or so. They only clean the outside. The inside is on you.

Washing Dishes

Although dishwashers are commonplace, many people still do the washing up (doing the dishes) by hand. Sinks have draining boards at the side so there is somewhere to stack your dishes. Not everyone rinses the soap off the dishes. This apparently horrifies the average American.

Doing the Washing

Brits say they are "doing their washing" rather than the laundry. Some still use clothes lines or rotary washing lines, either for environmental reasons, to keep costs down, or because clothes straight off the line smell nice and fresh.

Bedroom

If you're planning to spend many nights in the UK, you'll likely want to know that, compared to the US version, a king-size bed in the UK is considerably smaller than the US version.

Duvets and Duvet Covers

Although duvets with covers are available in the US, they are not as common as in the UK. In the US, a duvet refers to the cover. In the UK, the duvet is the inner part of a comforter and has a separate removable cover. The inner duvet is washed less frequently or taken to a dry cleaner. Duvets are too big for most British washing machines. Duvets are also known as quilts or the more dated term: continental quilts.

Bathroom

In the UK, a bathroom is the room where you take a bath. If you ask to use the bathroom, your host might think you need a good wash. Just ask if you can use the loo or toilet. Newer or updated houses may have an ensuite: that's a small bathroom or shower in the bedroom.

What's That String for?

It may surprise you to find a piece of string hanging from the ceiling at the entrance to the bathroom. This is a pull light switch. For safety reasons, British bathrooms do not have regular electrical sockets. You may see a two-pin (shaver) socket for use with small appliances such as toothbrushes and shavers. These have a transformer that only allows a small current, therefore making it safe to use near water. They will not accept or work with a more powerful appliance such as a hairdryer.

Electricity

Some Americans have inquired if British homes have electricity. We do, and it's twice as good as yours. OK, it's twice as powerful at 240 volts rather than 110. If you buy an adapter for your appliance to make it fit into the socket in the UK, that doesn't mean it will work. The adapter does not change the voltage. Someone who shall remain nameless bought their British girlfriend a "lady shave" from the PX on base in the UK. When plugged in, it blew a fuse and never worked again. This was a good outcome because she was considering sticking it where the sun doesn't shine. Thankfully, most appliances work on dual voltage, so your computer or phone should be fine with an adapter. But I'd recommend checking first.

A safety warning for your future relationships: Most women, whether American or British, do not find hair-removing tools an appropriate or romantic gift!

Telly and the Watershed

Watch British TV late in the evening and you will see images only available on subscription channels in the US. At 9 p.m., it's "watershed" (or unsuitable-for-children) time for telly viewers. Young children are expected to be in bed and it's time for the adults to watch telly. This means fewer restrictions on available content. Although most viewing is likely to be family friendly, you may want to make sure you are in control of the remote if you have children with you. Suddenly seeing a full-frontal nude might be a shock. On US TV, naked body parts are blurred out. In the UK, after the watershed, all bets are off. You will get to see the dangly bits in all their glory.

Box Sets

If a Brit asks you about your favorite box set, they are asking what you have been binge watching on a streaming service. A box set is a full series available online, a throwback to when people used to buy DVDs in physical box sets.

The BBC

The BBC provides commercial-free television, affectionately referred to as the "Beeb" or "Auntie Beeb." It is funded by a license fee. Though a political hot potato, it provides great value for the money. (See Troubleshooting for more on the license fee.)

Many shows you see on Netflix or US TV will have originated from the BBC or are in collaboration with them. They also fund a broad range of excellent commercial-free radio stations. Look for the BBC Sounds app on your phone, which doesn't currently require a license fee (except for some geographically restricted programming).

Want a Cuppa?

Visit a Brit at home and your host will offer you a cup of tea or coffee. This is not limited to people you know. If you have construction workers or installers visiting your home, they rarely will get down to work until you've made them a cuppa, usually with two sugars and preferably with a biscuit or three, known as builder's tea.

Tea is an institution. Strong, sweet tea for a shock (any event considered traumatic), tea for everyone when you need to sit down and thrash out an

argument, and tea when you are faced with any
situation where you aren't quite sure what to do next.
For the traditional experience, use a teapot and
maybe even use proper tea with tea leaves. To be
extra authentic, keep the pot warm with a tea cosy.
There are many types of tea, though breakfast tea
made from black tea leaves is most commonly
consumed.

The debate over whether you put the milk in before
the tea will run and run. For most reasonable people,
it's tea first. You must make sure it's the right color
before you add the milk. Weak, wishy-washy tea is a
food crime. Although there are some people who like
it that way, they are not to be trusted with any
decision-making.

You must also never make tea in a microwave. We
make tea with boiling water from a kettle—you
might know it as a teakettle. Every British home has
one. If someone asks you to put the kettle on, that
means fill with water and turn on the kettle to boil in
preparation for tea. It's usually a hint to say it's your
turn to make the tea. I know of one American who
put the kettle on by placing the electric kettle on the
hob (stovetop) and melted it. Don't do this.

You may hear the tea-making process referred to as
brewing, mashing (N) or steeping, depending on your
location. You must be careful not to leave the teabag
in the hot water for too long or you will stew the tea.

Dunking a biscuit in your tea is a very British habit.
You may have to practice finding the optimum point
for dunking before the biscuit dissolves and sinks to
the bottom of your cup. Some biscuits are more
suited to dunking than others.

Insults and Swear Words

HERE ARE some insults and swear words—some you must reserve for your sworn enemies, others you can playfully test out with your new friends. Do so at your own risk. Always check with someone you trust before dropping them into the conversation. Some of these will be acceptable in normal company, though there are exceptions. If you watch a certain type of British TV, you may erroneously believe that you can throw the "C" word around with abandon—not advisable. I have added a meaning where appropriate—most swear words don't mean anything.

Insults

D = Dated: You may hear them on older British TV programs.

Arsehole: Asshole

Arsewipe: Useless

Bag of shite: Good for nothing

Barmpot: Idiot (N)

Barmy: Slightly crazy

Bell end: The end of the penis

Berk: Idiot

Big Girl's Blouse: An insult questioning one's masculinity. (D)

Bollocks: Testicles

Bonkers: Crazy

Bugger: Generic, can be lighthearted

Bugger off: Go away

Buggerlugs: Can be affectionate

Chav: A low-class person who might wear fake designer clothes. (Think trailer trash. This is an insult.)

Cockwomble: Unpleasant or obnoxious

Crap: Rubbish

Dickhead: Dickhead

Dim: Stupid

Div: Idiot (N)

Dozy: Stupid

Face like a bag of spanners: Ugly

Fuckwit

Git: Commonly used with "old" (old git)

Gobshite: Loudmouth with nothing to say

Gormless: Stupid

Knobhead: Dickhead

Mardy: Bad tempered

Minger: Ugly

Muppet: Fool

Nincompoop: Stupid

Numbskull: Stupid

Numpty: Fool

Nutter: Crazy

Off your rocker: Not in your right mind

Pillock: Idiot

Piss artist: Drunkard

Pisshead: Drunkard

Pleb: Idiot (short for "plebian")

Potty: Stupid (D)

Prat: Idiot

Prick: Dick

Round the twist: Crazy (D)

Screwy: Crazy (D)

Shit for brains: Dumb

Silly bleeder: A generic insult similar to bugger.

Sod: Silly sod, cheeky sod

Toe rag: Lowlife

Toffee-nosed: Snobbish

Tosser: Jerk

Tosspot: Drunkard or generic insult.

Twat: Obnoxious

Twit: Idiot

Wally: Stupid (D)

Wanker: Someone who masturbates; a jerk

Wazzock: Stupid (N)

Swear Words

Balls
Blast
Bloody
Bloody hell
Damn and blast
Hell fire
Bollocks
Shite

The word "bloody" is common and rarely seen as offensive unless you are dealing with highly religious or uptight people. Similarly, "hell" is not seen as a swear word by most people.

Sayings and Slang

MOST OF THESE ARE SELF-EXPLANATORY. I have added examples to some for context.

Argue the toss: To pointlessly argue.

"I'm not going to argue the toss with you. That's just the way it is."

Argy bargy: An argument or loud dispute.

"Did you hear that argy bargy last night? I was watching through the net curtains."

Arse over tit: To fall or trip, often when drunk.

"He went arse over tit. I nearly spilled my pint!"

Aye: Yes (N)

Aye up: Hello (N)

A spot of: A bit. Brits might have a spot of tea or be in a spot of bother.

At loggerheads: To be in disagreement with someone.

"Our Brian is at loggerheads with Jim down the pub. He says he cheated at darts."

Bang to rights: Caught red-handed.

Banter: Friendly talk among friends; sometimes mildly offensive.

"Don't take offense. It's only a bit of banter, mate."

Billy-no-mates: Someone with no friends, often used as a self-deprecating term.

"I've got no one to go down to the pub with. I don't want to look like Billy-no-mates."

Blimey/cor-blimey: An expression of shock or surprise.

"Blimey. I didn't think he had it in him."

Blotted your copybook: Screwed up; messed up. (D)

Blow me/blow me down with a feather: Said when something surprises you (and not what you first thought).

Blue-arsed fly: Extremely busy.

"I've been running around like a blue-arsed fly all day."

Bob's your uncle: A way of saying, "It's finished" or "There it is."

"I promised I'd do it, and look, Bob's your uncle."

Bog standard: Ordinary

Brilliant: Used as an expression of joy, happiness, or excitement.

"You're having a baby? That's brilliant."

Can be used sarcastically. Roll your eyes and tut while saying "brilliant."

Cost a bomb: Expensive

Cheap as chips: Inexpensive

Chuffed/chuffed to bits: Extremely pleased. (N)

"I got invited to tea at Buckingham Palace. I'm chuffed to bits."

Crack on: Get on with it.

"I need to crack on. I've got a lot to do."

Daft: Stupid/dumb/idiotic. Can be used affectionately.

"Don't be daft. Put your money away. I'm buying this round."

A "do": Any event that includes a gathering of people.

"We're having a bit of a do on Friday. Can you make it?"

Dog's bollocks: Good.

"That new pub's the dog's bollocks."

Doing my head in: Annoying; frustrating.

"This spreadsheet is complicated. It's doing my head in."

"Will you stop going on? You are doing my head in."

Donkey's years: A lengthy period of time.

Doolally/doolally tap: Mentally not right.

Dropped a clanger: Messed up.

"He dropped a clanger and now we are in deep doodoo."

Every cloud: Taken from the saying, "Every cloud has a silver lining," yet said ironically.

"I lost my job, but now I watch telly all day. Every cloud, eh?"

Fantastic: Good or great.

"We had a fantastic holiday. Can't wait to go again."

Fit as a butcher's dog: "Fit" in this context means physically fit. Fit can also describe the perceived attractiveness of someone you fancy.

"He's well fit."

Flip your lid: Lose your temper.

Flounce: To leave dramatically, often after throwing a hissy fit.

Gammy leg: Generic term for something wrong with your leg that makes you unable to walk far or properly.

"I'd love to help with the sponsored walk, but I've got a gammy leg."

Get off with someone: Making out or more loosely hooking up or going on a date. (D)

"We went to the club, but she got off with that geezer with the dodgy eye."

Get off: Leave

"I have to get off now. I'll see you later."

Get sacked: Be fired from your job.

Gob: To spit on someone or something.

Gobsmacked: To be completely surprised by something.

"I found out he was fiddling the books. I was gobsmacked."

Happy as Larry: Extremely happy. (No, I don't know who Larry is.)

Hard cheese: Sucks to be you.

Hard lines: An unsympathetic response, similar to "Sucks to be you."

He's got some bottle: He's got balls or guts.

Her majesty's pleasure: Refers to someone in prison.

"She's detained at her majesty's pleasure."

Hoppit: Go away.

I'll give you a bell: I'll call you.

I'm all right, Jack: The worldview that says, "Sod everyone else as long as I'm OK."

It's a doddle: It's easy.

"This new computer system is a doddle to use."

It's not cricket: Not fair; unsportsmanlike.

It's not on: It's inappropriate/unfair/plain wrong.

"You can't do that. It's not on."

Jammy: Lucky

"The jammy bugger won the lottery, and he only started playing last week."

Jog on: Go away.

Jolly: Happy

Kicking off: A rise in tension sometimes leading to violence.

"She found out he'd been playing away with her best friend and now it's all kicking off."

Kicked into touch: Quit/dumped. Can refer to a person or an activity.

"I kicked smoking into touch years ago."

"I kicked him into touch when he started badmouthing my mates."

Knackered: Exhausted

Laters: Another way of saying goodbye.

Leg it: Run away.

Loads: A lot of something.

"I've done it loads of times before."

"She's got loads of money."

Lost the plot: Confused or lost the ability to do the job. Can also be used when someone is angry.

"The referee had completely lost the plot and was handing out red cards like Smarties."

Lost your bottle: Lost your courage.

"I was supposed to do a parachute jump, but I lost my bottle."

Lost your rag: Lost your temper.

Lumber: To dump responsibility on another person.

"He took the week off and lumbered me with all his work."

Mad as a box of frogs: Informally calling someone crazy or referring to someone who exhibits eccentric or odd behavior.

Made a pig's ear of it: To totally mess up.

"She decorated our wedding cake and made a right pig's ear of it."

Muckied your ticket: Screwed up, ruined your reputation. (N) (D)

Mustn't grumble/can't complain: An appropriate response if they ask you how you are.

Followed up with "Well, I could but nobody would care."

Mutton dressed as lamb: Refers to women of a certain age who should not wear clothes that are meant for a younger woman. It's of course offensive and sexist and thankfully is going out of fashion. Sometimes shortened to simply "mutton." (D)

Another old-fashioned phrase is "She's all fur coat and no knickers." A presumed slight at a woman who likes sex and also likes to dress well. (D)

Not my cup of tea: Not your thing.

Now then: An attention grabber.

"Now then, we need to have a talk."

In Yorkshire, "now then" is also a way of saying hello.

Off to: Going to/heading to.

"I'm off to the shops."

Off you go: Go ahead. Can be a dismissive way of saying "go away" or "get on with it."

Off your trolley: Behaving oddly or strangely.

"We all thought she was off her trolley leaving a good job to start a business."

On a promise: The hopeful expectation that you will have sexual relations in the very near future.

"I'm leaving early. He's coming for dinner and I'm on a promise."

Our: When referring to a family member.

"Our Brian's coming for his tea."

Pants: Rubbish.

"We waited all summer for the new movie. It turned out to be absolute pants."

Passable: Acceptable

"He made a passable attempt at ironing his shirt. It looked OK as long as he kept his jacket on."

Pear-shaped: To go wrong, often badly.

"The relationship started off well. It went pear-shaped when she discovered he didn't like cats."

Piece of piss: Easy.

"I thought the thousand-piece jigsaw would be a piece of piss until I discovered 900 pieces were blue sky."

Point Percy at the porcelain: Something gross and corny that a man might say when he's going for a pee.

"I'm off to point Percy (his dick) at the porcelain (the toilet)." (D)

Pretty: Used as a qualifier, i.e., it's pretty crap, pretty boring, a pretty stupid idea.

When used this way, it is rarely a compliment, although it is possible that someone could use the phrase "Pretty amazing." "Pretty good" is OK but not very good.

Proper: Another slang qualifier used in some communities.

"He's proper rich."

Pulling your leg: Telling an unbelievable story or untruth.

Pull the other one/it's got bells on: When someone believes you are pulling their leg or lying to them.

Put a sock in it: Shut up.

Quite: Quite pretty, quite good. (Not a great endorsement.)

Round the bend: Going a little crazy.

"I'm going round the bend trying to put up with the kids in the school holidays."

Rubbish: Garbage

"That was a rubbish film."

"I've just read the first draft of your report and it's a load of old rubbish."

Sack it off: Give up or quit.

Sandwich short of a picnic: Not all there/stupid.

Search me: I have no idea.

"Search me. I don't know where your car keys are."

See you later: Bye

This does not mean you will see the person again. It's just another way of saying goodbye.

Shanks' pony: To go on foot.

"I don't have a car, so I'll be coming on Shanks' pony."

Skint: Poor or having run out of money. Sometimes a temporary set of circumstances.

"She wants me to go on her hen night at a posh hotel, but I've just come back from my holidays and am skint."

Sod this for a game of soldiers: I'm done.

"We went camping, and it started pissing it down. I said, 'Sod this for a game of soldiers. I'm off to the pub.'"

Sod's Law: If something is likely to go wrong, it will go wrong. British version of Murphy's Law.

Spend a penny: To go to the toilet. Dates back to a time when you needed a penny to gain entrance to public toilets. (D)

Suited and booted: Dressed formally.

Sweet FA: Sweet Fanny Adams/fuck all. Said when you were expecting something and didn't get it.

"I stood all day at the car boot sale and made sweet FA for my trouble."

Ta-ra: Goodbye. (N)

Ta: Thanks. (N)

Takes the cake or takes the biscuit: Outstandingly good or bad.

"He came to work three hours late on his first day. That takes the cake."

Taking the mickey/mick: To make fun of.

Teach your grandma to suck eggs: To patronize someone who knows more than you. (D)

Throw a wobbly: To have a meltdown.

Tight as a duck's arse: Cheap

Tits up: To go horribly wrong.

"He started dating a woman at work, but it all went tits up."

Toddle off: Move along.

Toodlepip: Goodbye

Touching cloth: When you need to poop and it's nearly popping out of your bum.

"I need to go home. I'm touching cloth."

Tough as old boots: Strong in character or physically tough; can also refer to inanimate objects.

"We will use my old tent for camping, but don't worry. It's tough as old boots."

Up the spout: Messed up.

What's he like?/What are you like?: Said when someone is doing something surprising or that you don't agree with but don't have the guts to challenge.

"Oh, that's a bit racist. What are you like?"

The correct response? "Stop being a racist arsehole."

What's occurring: What's happening?

A phrase popularized in the TV series *Gavin and Stacey*.

Where there's muck, there's brass: The belief that getting one's hands dirty leads to financial success. (N)

Wind yer neck in: Calm down. Keep your nose out.

Winding someone up: Joking, kidding. Telling them something unbelievable, or that they don't want to hear, can be done in the form of a prank.

"I told him I was quitting the football team, but I was only winding him up."

Winding me up: Said when you don't believe what the person is telling you.

"The tickets to the gig are two hundred quid? You're winding me up, right?"

Y'all right?/You all right?: If someone inquires as to any of the above, they are not requesting your medical or personal history. Similar to asking "What's up," the correct answer is to respond in kind. The person is merely greeting you.

If said with a specific inflection that sounds more like a question, maybe you are looking like a moody bugger and they are indeed worried that you are not all right. You can then say, "I'm fine" in a quietly passive-aggressive way.

Yer (you're) having a laugh: A response to a ludicrous suggestion.

"He offered me 10 quid to give him a lift home. I said, 'Yer having a laugh. It's miles away. Get a taxi.'"

You don't know your arse from your elbow: You have no clue what you are talking about.

You know what I mean?: Sometimes sounds like "Ya nat I mean." Another phrase that can come at the end of any sentence and is mostly rhetorical.

"I worked hard, and they fired me anyway. You know what I mean?"

Up himself, up yourself: Taking yourself too seriously.

"She's really up herself now she's married that toff."

British Word List

REMEMBER the British word is listed first.

A

A and E (accident and emergency): Emergency room, previously known as Casualty.

A-Z Maps: Street map in paperback or spiral-bound book for a specific town. Though most people use their phones for directions, A-Z Maps are still available in print and can be useful in unfamiliar areas.

Abseiling: Rappeling

Academic staff: Faculty

Ace: A dated way of saying "good" or "cool."

Action man: Male action figure similar to GI Joe.

Aerial: Antenna

Aggro: Aggravation

Airing cupboard: A cupboard where you keep linens, usually warm because it is in the same place as the water heater. A place to put laundered clothes that are almost dry, possibly after being hung on the line.

Alight: To get off a train or bus.

Allotment: A small piece of land that individuals may rent from the local city or authority to grow their own produce. Although it will be in an area that has multiple allotments, yours is your own and not community owned. They are popular with those who live in flats (apartments). They became popular after the war.

Anorak: A person who behaves in a nerdy fashion.

Anorak: Rain jacket

Anti-clockwise: Counter-clockwise

Arse: Ass

Arsehole: Asshole

Asian: When Brits refer to Asians, they usually mean people from South Asia (i.e., India, Pakistan, Bangladesh).

Aubergine: Eggplant

Autocue: Teleprompter

Autumn: Fall

B

Bag for life: Reusable carrier bag. (See Shopping and single-use, plastic-bag rules)

Bagsy: Claim dibs

BAME: Black and Minority Ethnic

Banged up: Locked up

Banging: Good or excellent

Banter: Friendly teasing, being made fun of.

Barge pole: Ten-foot pole

Barrister: A solicitor/lawyer qualified to advocate in higher courts.

BBQ: Grill

Bedside table/bedside cabinet: Nightstand

Bedsit: A one-room flat with shared facilities.

Beefeaters: The Yeomen Warders with the furry hats who guard the Royal Palace and the Tower of London. It's not cool to heckle them. They are trained not to respond.

Beer garden: An outside area of a pub that allows children; allows families to eat and drink together.

Bee's knees: Great, fabulous, awesome.

Belisha beacon: Amber lights that flash at a road's pedestrian crossing area.

Bender: A heavy drinking session.

Bespoke: Customized

Bevvy: An alcoholic beverage.

Big Ben: Often assumed to be the famous clock. Big Ben is the bell of the clock at the palace of Westminster. The "bongs" of the bell identify the official time and are used to signal the start of the news on some TV news programs.

Big light: The main ceiling light in a living room. Originally a Northern saying; now more widespread. (Referred to by comedian Peter Kay and his "Put Big Light On" skit.)

"Put the big light on. I need to sign this check."

Blighty: Britain

Bloke: Man

Blouse: A woman's shirt

Blow out: Blow dry

Blower: Telephone

"Get him on the blower and tell him to sort it."

Blues and twos: Referring to the blue lights and dual sirens of an emergency vehicle when responding to a call.

Boarding school: It's not just in Harry Potter. People do still go away to live at school.

Bobbins: Crap/rubbish

"It was bobbins."

Bobble: Hair tie

Bobby: Affectionate term for a police officer. (D)

Bobby dazzler: Good looking. (D)

Bodge: Do something in a sloppy manner.

Boffin: A scientist, nerd or brain box.

Bog: An impolite word for the toilet.

Bollards: Road separators made of concrete or metal.

Bombay mix: A spicy mix of nuts and/or seeds. Once seen as an upscale alternative to crisps to serve at parties.

Bonk: Have sex

Boozer: Pub

Boxing Day: Bank holiday the day after Christmas. (See Holiday section.)

Braces: Suspenders

Brackets: Parentheses

Brass: Money

Brass monkey weather: Cold weather. From the saying "Cold enough to freeze the balls off a brass monkey."

Break time: Recess

Brekky: Breakfast

Bridleway: Footpath

Brownies: Similar to young Girl Scouts.

Brush: Broom

Budge: Move

"Can you budge up a bit? I need some more room."

Bugger all: Nothing

"I've got bugger all done today."

Building society: Bank similar to a credit union.

Bum: Butt

Bum bag: Fanny pack

Bumph: Unnecessary paperwork

Bunting: Flags. (The small colorful type connected with string that you hang outside for celebrations.)

Burgle: Burglarize

Bureau de change: Currency exchange

Butty: Sandwich (N)

C

Car boot (trunk) sale: Yard sale/flea market. Held in a field where they charge a fee to park your car. Vendors sell items from the car boot (trunk). They may also bring tables and displays.

Caretaker: Janitor

Cashier: Teller

Casualty: Older term for an emergency room.

Central reservation: Median

Checkout: Cash register

Cheeky monkey: Calling someone a "cheeky monkey" or "little monkey" is a term of endearment. It is not race related. There are some words that are used differently, and this is one of them. We usually use it when talking to children, though on some occasions it might be used for an adult. It is unlikely to have any racial undertones.

Cheeky: Impertinent, but can be humorous.

"He asked me to buy him a pint, the cheeky sod."

Cheerio: Bye

Cheesy: Corny

Chemist: Pharmacy

Cheque: Check

Chest of drawers: Dresser/drawer chest

Childminder: Professional babysitter who cares for children in their own home.

Chinwag: Chat

"Let's have a chinwag."

Chippy: Carpenter (slang).

Chippy: The fish-and-chip shop.

Chock-a-block/chocka: Full.

"The shops were chock-a-block during the Boxing Day sale."

Chuffed/chuffed to bits: Thrilled

Cling film: Saran Wrap

Clink: Prison

Clothes horse: Wooden or plastic frame for air-drying clothes.

Cobblers: Shoe repairer

Cobbles/cobblestones: Rounded stone blocks used in roads. Also refers to the road itself. Although old-fashioned, they are still common in some areas of England.

"We walked on the cobbles."

Colleague: Co-worker

Compere: Master of ceremonies

Compo: Compensation (usually paid in relation to a civil lawsuit).

Congestion charge: A fee you must pay if you drive into London.

Conservatory: Sunroom often added to a house after construction.

Contraflow: Diversions with traffic cones on a motorway.

Cooker: Oven

Copper: Policeman or woman

Corner shop: Convenience store

Coronation Street: Long-running soap opera set among the cobbles of a Lancashire street and the Rovers Return pub.

Corridor: Hallway

Cot: Crib

Council house: Rented public housing

Court shoes: Pumps

Cowboy builder: Tradesman who cheats, overcharges or does shoddy work. Cowboy can be used for anyone who does crappy work or takes advantage of others.

Crazy golf: Miniature golf

Creche: Nursery or daycare sometimes provided by employers.

Crimbo: Christmas

Crossroads: Intersection

Cuddly toy: Soft toy

Cupboard: Closet or kitchen cupboard

Curling tongs: Curling irons

Current account: Checking account

Curriculum Vitae (CV): Resume

Curtains: Drapes

Cushy: Easy

Cutlery: Silverware

D

Dear: Expensive

Detached house: A single-family home on its own land unattached to other dwellings.

Dodgy: Untrustworthy

Dodgems: Bumper cars (at the fairground).

Dogging: If you ever get invited to do this, remember it has nothing to do with your four-legged friend. Dogging means having sex in public places with an audience. There really is something for everyone, isn't there?

Dole: Unemployment

Doo-doo: Feces

Dosh: Money

Doss: To not do very much.

"He's a dosser. He never does any work."

Double-barreled: Having two surnames separated by a hyphen.

Dowdy: Dull, often referring to clothes or appearance.

Draughts: Checkers

Drawing pin: Thumb tack

Dressing gown: Bathrobe

Dummy: Pacifier

Durex: Brand name of a condom.

Dust cart: Garbage truck

Dustman: Garbage man

Dustpan and shovel: Dustpan and broom

Duvet: Comforter. (See Homes section.)

Driving Words and Terms

Amber traffic light: Yellow light

Bonnet: Hood

Boot: Trunk

Car park: Parking lot

Crossroads: Intersection/four-way stop

Dipped headlights: Low beam

Dual carriageway: Divided highway

Full beam: High beam

Handbrake: Parking brake

Heavy Goods Vehicle Driver (HGV Driver): Truck driver

Heavy Goods Vehicle (HGV): Truck

Indicator: Turn signal

Lorry: Truck

MOT: Mandatory annual road test for vehicles, previously administered by the Ministry of Transport, now by the Department for Transport.

Motor: Car

Motorbike: Motorcycle

Motorway: Interstate

Pavement: Sidewalk

People carrier: SUV

Petrol: Gas

Reversing lights: Backup lights

Roundabout: Turning circle

Saloon car: Sedan

Sleeping policeman: Speed bump

Slip road (motorways): On/off ramp

Taxi: Cab

Tyre: Tire

Windscreen: Windshield

Wing mirror: Side mirror

Write off: A car deemed "cannot be repaired" by the insurance company after an accident.

Written off: Totaled

E

Earthed: Grounded (electrical)

Earwig: Eavesdrop

"He was earwigging all the time we were talking."

EastEnders: Soap opera set in the East End of London.

Egg-and-spoon race: A race traditionally during school sports days where the participant balances an egg on a spoon while running.

Elbow grease: Hard work/effort

"You will need to use some elbow grease to get that yard cleaned up."

Emersion heater: Hot water heater

Em: Slang for "them."

"I don't like 'em."

Estate agent: Realtor

Estate car: Station wagon

Ethnic minority: An ethnic racial group not part of the majority in a country. Often used to describe immigrant communities.

Extension lead: Extension cord

F

Faff around: Procrastinate, to take too long in getting to the point.

"I didn't get anything done as I was faffing around all day."

Faffy: Intricate, detailed, taking longer than expected.

Fag: Cigarette

Fantastic: Great/wonderful/fabulous

Fairy lights: Christmas lights

Fancy: Physically attracted to someone.

"I think you fancy that fit bloke from down the street." (D)

Fancy dress: Costume. Worn by Americans on Halloween. Can be used as an insult.

"Are you really wearing that? I thought you were in fancy dress."

Fancy dress party: Costume party

Fiddly: Hard to do, awkward, requiring attention to detail.

"I need to paint my door, but it has so many windows it will be a fiddly job."

Film: Movie

Fire brigade: Fire department

Fit: Attractive, good looking, sexy. (Has nothing to do with actual fitness.) (D)

Fiver: Five pounds

Flannel: Washcloth

Flash: To expose one's genitals to someone.

Flasher: The person doing the flashing.

Flat: Apartment

Flatmate: Roommate

Flex: Electrical cord

Flog: To sell

"I'm going to flog this watch; I need the money."

Fluke: A lucky or unexpected outcome.

Foisty: Musty

Football pitch: Football field

Footie: Football

Fortnight: Two weeks

"I'm going on my holidays for a fortnight."

Foyer: Lobby

Freefone/freephone: Toll-free number

Fringe: Bangs

Full English: Cooked breakfast

Full Stop: Period (as in the end of a sentence).

Fully inclusive holiday: A package holiday that includes hotel, transport, food, alcoholic drinks and entertainment.

Fuzz: Police

G

Gaffer tape: Duct tape

Garden: Yard

Geezer: Man

Gen up: Research

Geordie: Person from Tyneside, Northeast England.

Goolies: Testicles

Goose pimples: Goose bumps

Gnashers: Teeth

Gob: Mouth

General Practitioner (GP): Doctor

A grand: A thousand pounds.

Grass: To snitch on someone.

Green fingers: Green thumb

Grey: Gray

Grill: Broil

Grit bin: A bin at the end of your road filled to sprinkle your snowy/icy path. Mainly found in an area of high elevation or an area that gets blocked by ice and snow.

Gritter: Truck that spreads grit/rock salt on icy roads in the winter.

"The gritters are out, it must be going to snow."

Gumption: Initiative

Gutted: Deeply disappointed

"My team lost, and I'm gutted."

The gods: The highest part of a theater.

"I could only get us tickets way up in the gods. I hope you don't get nosebleeds."

Guv/Guv'nor: Boss

H

Hair slide/clip: Barrette

Half-term: A holiday, usually a week off from school or college in the spring and autumn, similar to spring break.

Hand luggage: Carry-on bag

Handbag: Purse

Hard: Tough

"He's really hard. Don't mess with him."

Hash sign: Pound sign or hashtag. Can be confusing because the pound sign refers to currency= £.

Hay fever: Seasonal allergies

Headmaster/headteacher: Principal

Heaving: Busy or crowded

"I went to the pub. It was heaving."

Hen night: Bachelorette party

Higgledy-piggledy: All mixed up/upside down.

"I need to tidy up. My clothes are all higgledy-piggledy in my drawers."

High street: Main street

Hob: Stove

Holdall: Sports-type bag often used in small bank robberies, or possibly weekends away. If they feature a holdall in a British TV show, there will not be a good outcome.

Holiday: Vacation

Hoover: Vacuuming. (A brand name that became the generic word for vacuuming.)

Hot flushes: Hot flashes

Hundreds and thousands: Sprinkles

I

Identity parade: Police lineup

Inverted commas: Quotation marks

Invigilator: Proctor

Ironmonger: Hardware store

J

Jabs: Vaccinations

Jacksie: Ass

"Get off your jacksie and do some work."

Jobcentre: Employment office

Jobsworth: Someone who is unhelpful or inflexible in their duties.

"It's more than my job's worth."

Jollies: Holidays, or it can refer to something you enjoy doing.

Jug: Pitcher

Jumble sale: Rummage/garage sale

Jump leads: Jumper cables

Jumper: Sweater

K

Karzie: Toilet

Keks/kecks: Trousers

Kerb: Curb

Keyhole surgery: Laparoscopic surgery

Kip: Sleep or nap

Kit: Equipment/gear/uniform

"Remember to bring your football kit."

Kitchen roll: Paper towel

Knees up: Party

Knickers: Panties. Brits don't use the word "panties," and saying it can seem pervy and weird because the only place it's used is in porn or by sleaze balls.

Knuckle-duster: Brass knuckle

L

L plates (learner plates): Learner (beginning) drivers must display this plate on their car until they pass their driving test.

Ladybird: Ladybug

Landing: Top of the stairs.

Lass: Girl

Lav (lavatory): Toilet

Lead: Leash (used to walk your dog).

Leaflet: Flyer

Learnt: Learned

Lift: Elevator

Lift: Ride. (To give someone a lift.)

Lingerie: Intimate apparel

Lob: Throw

"Lob me the remote."

Lock-in: A gathering at a pub after legal licensing hours. The licensee's friends are often invited to stay after the pub has closed. It is legal only if drinks are given as gifts and not sold.

Lodger: Renter

Lollipop (lolly): Sucker

Lollipop man/lady: School crossing guard

Loo: Toilet

Lout: Thug

Love bite: Hickey

Lurgy: Sickness/germs

"Don't come near me if you've got the lurgy."

M

Magpie: Common black-and-white bird. Superstition says "one for sorrow, two for joy," so you always want to see two together.

Main course: Entrée

Mains: Electric power supply

"I think a fuse has blown; you better turn the power off at the mains."

Maisonette: Apartment block/tenement (D)

Managing director: Chief operating officer

Manky: Dirty

Marquee: A large tent, the kind where you might hold a wedding or outdoor event.

Mate: Friend. (A term of affection even though they are not actually your mates.)

"Thanks, mate. Y'all right, mate. Cheers, mate."

Maths: Math

Meat and two veg: A traditional meal. Also slang for a man's genitals.

Metric system: The system of measurement in the UK.

Miffed: Annoyed or irritated

Mint condition (shortened to "mint"): Perfect condition

Mobile: Cell phone

Moulting: Shedding

"Keep your dog away from me. It's moulting and I've got my best suit on."

Muck rake: Stir up trouble or dig up information on someone. (D)

Mucky: Dirty

Mum: Mom. Though Mum is the most common shortened word for mother, there are regional variations.

Mam: Sometimes used in the North of England.

Mams: Another version of mom, this time in Wales.

Mom: Sometimes used in areas around Birmingham and the Midlands of England.

Mummy: Used in the South of England/London.

Other uses depending on location are Ma, Mummy and Mother.

Metric and Measurements

The UK uses the metric system for weights and measures. Americans still measure in feet and inches. NOTE: The British spelling for metric measurements ends in "re" (i.e., kilometre, metre, litre).

Metric Conversion

Kilometer: 1 Kilometer = 0.62 of a mile

Meter: 1 Meter = 3 feet, 3 inches

Centimeter: 1 Centimeter = 0.39 inches

Kilogram: 1 Kilogram = 2.2 pounds

Liter: 1 Liter = 1 3/4 pints

Stones

Brits use "stones" (st) as a unit measuring their weight. Of course, we don't have a pile of heavy rocks in our bathroom to compare our weight to, though British weighing scales do measure in stones. A stone is 14 pounds. If a Brit says they lost 5 stone (they refer to it in the singular, never 5 *stones*), that doesn't mean they were wandering through the woods dropping rocks out of their pocket like a Hansel and Gretel story. It means they lost a considerable amount of weight. You may see diet plans promising that you will drop a stone in a month, and a seven-stone-weakling is an insult. Many dieters have an aspirational stone weight they want to reach as their goal. To be 8st 13 pounds sounds way better that 9st.

Temperature

The UK uses the Celsius temperature scale.

21.1 Celsius equals 70 degrees Fahrenheit. Water freezes at 0 degrees and boils at 100.

Beer is served in pints. A UK pint is slightly bigger than a US one, as is a gallon.

N

999: Emergency number, like 911.

Naff: Tacky

Nappy: Diaper

Natter: Chatter

Netball: Similar to basketball, mainly played by schoolgirls.

Net curtains: Thin, lacy or mesh-style curtains that hang close to the window behind the regular curtains. You can peek through your nets and spy on your neighbors without them seeing you.

Nick: Steal

Nicking: Stealing

Nicked: Stolen

Nicked: Arrested

"You're nicked, son."

Nil: Zero

Nipper: Child

Nippy: Cold

Nits: Head lice

No comment: Plead the fifth.

Nought: Zero

Noughts and crosses: Tic Tac Toe

Nous/e: Common sense

"Use your nous."

Nowt: Nothing (Y)

Number plate: License plate

O

Old Age Pensioner (OAP): Senior

Off license (offie): Liquor store

Old banger: Dilapidated car, a hooptie (slang).

Old bill: Police

On your tod: On your own (Y)

Open day: Open house

Outskirts: Suburbs

Overalls: Dungarees

Overleaf: Reverse/other side of the page

"Continues overleaf."

Owt: Anything (Y)

Ow do: Hello (Y)

P

Package holiday: Vacation package that includes flights, accommodations and transport.

Packed lunch: Bag lunch

Pants: Underwear

Pantomime: A particularly British family show. Men and women play interchangeable gender roles for some of the parts. Normally performed at Christmas with fading celebrities in starring roles. Although cheesy, they are popular and are often a child's first introduction to theater. If you attend a pantomime as an adult without desiring to poke one's own eyes out, I salute you.

Paracetamol: Acetaminophen (like Tylenol).

Paraffin: Kerosene

Parcel: Package

Parky: Cold

"It's a bit parky out there. You better put a coat on." (Y)

Pavement: Sidewalk

Pelican crossing/zebra crossing: A crosswalk, often with flashing lights. (See Belisha beacon.)

Perspex: Plexiglass

Phone box: Phone booth

Pictures: Cinema/movies. (Old term still in use, especially in the North).

"We're off to the pictures."

Piles: Hemorrhoids

Pillar box: Red post box

Pinch: Steal

Not to be confused with pinching someone's bum, which is sexual assault.

Pinny (pinafore): Apron (D)

Plaster: Band-Aid

Plasterboard: Drywall

Play truant: Skip class

Playtime: Recess at school

Plectrum: Guitar pic

Plod: Slang for a police officer.

Plot of land: Parcel of land

Podiatrist: Foot doctor

Points: Railway switch

"The train will be late because of a points failure."

Polo neck jumper: Turtleneck sweater

Pong: Unpleasant smell

Poorly: Sick

Pop your clogs: Die

Poppycock: Nonsense

Porridge: Time spent in prison

Posh: Fancy/upscale

Post: Mail

Postage and packing: Shipping and handling

Postcode: ZIP code

Postman: Mailman

Pound shop: Dollar store

Posidriv/posidrive: Generic term used for any Phillips screwdriver.

Prang: Dent or damage

"The silly tosser pranged my new car."

Press studs: Snaps

Press-ups: Push-ups

Pressie: Present

Primary school: Elementary school

Promenade (prom): Boardwalk

Pukka: Legitimate, the real deal.

Puncture: Flat tire

Punter: Customer/client/user of services

Pupil: Student

Pushchair: Stroller

Q

Quack: A doctor with questionable qualifications.

Queue: Line. Brits like queuing; they do it for everything. Make sure you don't try to "jump" the queue because they take them very seriously.

Quid: Pound

Quids in: Being in a financially good position.

R

Rambling: Walking/hiking

Randy: Horny

Recce: Recon to check something out in advance, reconnaissance. From the French term "reconnoiter."

Received Pronunciation (RP): A refined accent previously used on TV and by the upper classes.

Reception desk: Front desk

Recorded delivery: Certified mail

Redundant: Lose your job. (Usually when a company closes, downsizes or your job is no longer required.) Not the same as being fired.

"They made me redundant."

Reel of cotton: Spool of thread

Registry/registry office: Where births, deaths and marriages are recorded.

Removal van: Moving van

Rent: Hire

Return ticket: Round-trip ticket

Revise: Study for an exam or test.

Ribbing: Similar to banter, friendly teasing.

Ring: Call

"Give me a ring when you're ready to go down to the pub.

Rizlas: Brand name of cigarette rolling papers used generically.

Road: Street

Roadworks: Construction

"Don't drive that way. There's roadworks."

Ropey: Poor quality; a way to describe awful food.

Rounders: A game played by children in parks, suspiciously similar to baseball.

Row: Argument

"We had a row, and she's really pissed off."

Rubber: Eraser

Rubbish: Garbage/trash

Rucksack: Backpack

Rumpy-pumpy: Sexual intercourse

S

Sacked: Fired

Sarky: Sarcastic

SAS (Special Air Service): Military unit similar to the Green Berets.

Satnav: GPS

Schedule: Same spelling but sounds like shedule.

Scouser: Someone from Liverpool.

Scrap: Junk

Sea: Ocean

Seaside: Oceanside or beach

Secateurs: Pruning scissors

Secondment: Being seconded or on secondment. When your employer temporarily sends you to work in another part of the organization or branch. (It can be a positive, an opportunity to work in a new place or learn a new skill. Or it might be that your boss wants to get rid of you for a while because you've been a bit of a dosser.)

Sell-by date: Expiration date on food.

Sellotape: Scotch tape

Semi-detached house: Duplex

Service station: Rest stop

Serviette: Napkin

Settee: Sofa

Shag: Have sex

Shagged: Tired

Shirty: Irritated or angry

Shoddy: Cheaply made or badly done; shoddy workmanship.

Shop: Store

Shopping center: Shopping mall

Shufty: Look

"Let's have a shufty at the new baby then."

Sixes and sevens: Discombobulated

Six of one and half a dozen of the other: It's all the same thing.

Six weeks' holiday: School summer break

Skew-whiff: Cock-eyed, not straight.

Skint: Broke

Skip: Dumpster

Skive: To avoid work or duties.

Slag off: To speak badly about someone.

Sleeping partner: Silent partner in a business.

Slowcoach: Slowpoke

Skirting boards: Baseboards

Smalls: Underwear

Smarmy: Creepy or untrustworthy.

Smart: Well-dressed

Smashing: Wonderful

"He's a smashing bloke."

SME (small- and medium-size enterprise): Small business

Smoke (The): London

Smithereens: Tiny pieces

"He dropped the vase and it smashed into smithereens."

Snog: Kiss

Socket (electric): Outlet

Solicitor: Lawyer

Sorted: Fixed, done, completed, organized. (Does not mean alphabetically sorted.)

"Have you ordered the stationery for the event?" "Yes, it's sorted."

"I have sorted the food for the party."

Sound: Good/excellent (D)

Spade: Shovel

Spanner: Wrench

Spark out/sparko: Fast asleep

Splash out: Spend a sizable amount of money or buy something expensive.

Spliff: Joint/blunt

Spots: Pimples

Spunk: Semen

Squaddie: A military grunt

Squidgy: Soft and squishy

Staffroom: Teachers' lounge

Stag night: Bachelor party

Stanley knife: Box cutter

Star jumps: Jumping jacks

Starkers: Naked

Starter: Appetizer

Strides: Trousers

Stilettos: High-heel shoes

Stocky: Heavy/fat

Stone: Unit of measurement for weight. 1 stone=14 pounds. British weighing scales use stones. (See Metric and Measurements section.)

Straight away: Immediately

Strimmer: Weedwacker

Stroppy: Bad-tempered

Suss out: Figure out

"He sussed that I was lying."

Swear: Curse

Sweary: Using curse words.

Sweets: Candy

Sweetshop: Candy store

Swimsuit/swimming   **costume/cozzie** **(slang):**

Bathing suit

Swot: Study for a test. (Can be a noun.)

T

Tram: Streetcar

Table football: Foosball

Takings: Business receipts

"He took the takings to the bank."

Tablet: Pill

Tailback: Traffic jam. (Usually a long line of traffic from one junction to the next on a motorway.)

Takeaway: Takeout/carryout (food)

Tap: Faucet

Tat: Junk or stuff you might buy in a souvenir shop while on holiday.

Tatty: Old/worn/in poor condition

Ta-ra: Bye (N)

Tea towel: The cloth you use to dry your dishes after handwashing.

Telly: Television

Tenner: Ten pounds

Term: Semester

Terraced house: Row house

Three lions on a shirt: Symbol of the England football team.

Throw a wobbly: Have a meltdown; lose your temper.

Tick: Check ✔

Ticket tout: Scalper

Tidy/tidy up: To straighten up/clear away. ("Tidy" has many other meanings, such as a tidy sum means a lot of money.)

Tidgy: Tiny

Tight: Cheap

"He was so tight, he brought his own drinks to the pub."

Tights: Pantyhose

Till: Cash register

Till roll: Paper receipt roll. (Always runs out just when it's your turn to pay.)

"Hang on a minute, love. My till roll's run out."

Timetable: Schedule

Tin: Can

Tippex (brand): Wite-Out liquid paper corrector.

Telling Time

Five to: Five minutes to the hour. 4:55 p.m.

Ten to: Ten minutes to the hour. 4:50 p.m.

Quarter to: Fifteen minutes to the hour. 4:45 p.m.

Twenty to: Twenty minutes to the hour. 4:40 p.m.

Five past: Five minutes past the hour. 5:05 p.m.

Ten past: Ten minutes past the hour. 5:10 p.m.

Quarter past: Fifteen minutes past the hour. 5:15 p.m.

Twenty past: Twenty minutes past the hour. 5:20 p.m.

Half past: 30 minutes past the hour. 5:30 p.m.

Toff: Insulting name for a rich or upper-class person.

Todger: Penis

Toilet: Restroom. If you are looking for a public toilet, look for the sign "Toilets" or "WC." (You may notice that toilets do not have huge gaps above and below the doors. Toilet doors generally are fully closed. Don't get yourself locked in because you won't be able to crawl out from under.)

Tomato sauce: Ketchup

Top up: Refill. You "top up" your mobile phone credit. At the pub, you might ask for your beer to be topped up.

Torch: Flashlight

Tower block: High-rise apartment

Trainers: Running shoes/sneakers

Tracky: Tracksuit

Tracky bottoms: Sweatpants

Training wheels: Stabilizers

Tramp: Homeless person or vagrant

Tranny: Radio (from transistor radio) (D)

Transport cafe: Truck stop

Truncheon/nightstick: Police officer's weapon

Turf accountant: Bookmaker/bookie

Turning/turn: An easy-to-miss turn in the road, usually off the main road.

"Take the third turn on the right after the pub on the corner."

Treat (sounds like "tret"): Treat, or how one is taken care of.

"He treat me really well."

Triple: Treble

Trousers: Pants

Trump: To break wind or fart. (Often used by children.)

Twig or twig on: Catch on/figure out

"I think he finally twigged what we are up to."

The Tube: London underground or subway

U

Umpteen: A lot/many

"I've told you umpteen times to stop kicking that ball against my wall."

Underground: Subway

Underpants: Men's underwear

Uni: University

Union Jack/Union Flag: National flag of the United Kingdom. The official name is the Union Flag. (Only called the Union Jack when on a ship, though in practice it's still mostly referred to as the Union Jack.)

Up sticks: Pull up stakes, leave town.

V

Vest: Undershirt

W

WC (abbreviation for water closet): Toilet or bathroom

Waffle: To speak at length, ramble on while saying nothing much.

Waistcoat: Vest

Wangle: Persuade or manipulate

"He wangled himself an upgrade."

Wardrobe: Closet

Washing-up liquid: Dish soap

Washing: Laundry

Watford Gap: Motorway service station at the Northamptonshire/Warwickshire border; the unofficial boundary separating North and South England. If you are North of Watford Gap, you are deemed to be in the North.

Wedding tackle: Men's genitals

Wee: Pee

Wellington boots (wellies): Rain boots/rubber boots

Wheel brace: Lug wrench

Wheelie bin: Trash can

Whinge: Moan/complain

Whip-round: Monetary collection to buy a gift for a colleague or friend.

Wonky: Lopsided, not as it should be, similar to skew whiff.

Wot: What. Said loudly and aggressively. (Popular phrase in the British soap opera *EastEnders*.)

X Is for Kisses

Brits put kisses in greeting cards and text messages. It doesn't mean they want to put their tongue down your throat. It just means they are being friendly.

Y

Y-fronts: Men's underwear. (Similar to tighty whities.)

Y'all right? You OK?: This is a rhetorical question.

Yak: Talking incessantly.

"Stop yakking on at me."

Yank: American. It doesn't matter where in the US you come from, to many Brits you will always be a Yank.

Yank: To pull harshly.

"He yanked my arm."

Yob: Hooligan

Yonks: An interminable period.

"It's been yonks since I've seen you.

Z

Zebra crossing: Pedestrian crossing

Z (pronounced "zed"): The letter Z

Zero-hours contract: A work contract with no guarantee of hours, which is mostly despised by working people.

Zimmer frame: Walker

Zip: Zipper

Zonked: Exhausted

Troubleshooting

NOW THAT YOU are more familiar with life in the UK, this chapter covers information on avoiding any potential pitfalls.

Avoid These Phrases and Actions

Though you are unlikely to say most of these, you don't know what you don't know. There may be one or two you weren't aware could be offensive.

"Everything is small and old."

"I thought it would be bigger, cleaner, brighter, less expensive, more like a postcard."

Brits have pride, too. Though they might enjoy hearing what you like about their country, they will be less keen to hear criticism. Yes, some things are smaller, yet it is a stereotype and the punch line to many old jokes about Americans. You don't want to sound like a punch line.

"I'm Scottish, Welsh or Irish."

Unless you were actually born there or can show strong links to your heritage, this one should be avoided.

"Are you from London?" Similar to how not everyone in the US lives in Washington, D.C., London is just one city. Familiarize yourself with a map so that when people tell you where they are from, you might have an idea where it is located.

Don't do British accents. You will probably sound like Dick Van Dyke in *Mary Poppins* and no one will be impressed.

"Do you know John who lives in Liverpool?"

There are more than 50 million people in the UK. They don't all know the queen or your friend who moved to the Cotswolds in 1997.

"Why don't you have air conditioning?"

In the UK, they only need air conditioning twice a year and it's not worth the expense.

Never order an "Irish Car Bomb" or anything similarly named.

Although a popular drink in some parts of the US—and you might even have been served one in an Irish bar—it is offensive to many people with knowledge of Irish history. Car bombs are not seen as a fun name for a drink.

The V Sign

Be wary of using your fingers to indicate the number two. In Britain, raising two fingers with the back of the hand facing outward has a similar meaning to giving the middle finger.

Brexit

The controversial vote for Britain to exit the European Union has divided families and friends and caused people to become firmly entrenched in their views. It's probably best to avoid this discussion unless you are sure of your audience's viewpoint.

Politics

Politics has become as extremely divisive in the UK as it has in the US. It is unlikely you will make friends by having strong, uninformed opinions. Stay clear of hot-button issues. Talk about the weather.

The 'G' Word

Brits may have a curiosity about your gun collection, but it is more likely that you will come across as an arsehole if you bring it up without knowing your audience. Think of a gun like a dick. If you have one, unless someone specifically inquires about it, don't talk about it, share photos of it, wave it around, or push it in people's faces.

Solutions to Common Problems

None of the outlets will work.

British outlets (sockets) usually have an on/off switch. If you don't turn it on, your appliance will not work.

The food in the store is out of date.

Dates in the UK are arranged by day/month/year. If an item has a sell-by date of 01/12/2022, it is 1 December 2022. Bear this in mind if you are asked for your date of birth.

I burned my hand on the scalding water in the sink.

You may find individual hot and cold water "taps," though some will have US-style mixer faucets. Put the plug in the sink and fill it with water to the temperature that you prefer.

I asked for ice and they only gave me one chunk.

As sodas are not generally offered with free refills, half filling a glass with ice before adding soda feels like you are being cheated.

They say I will go to jail for watching TV.

The BBC is publicly funded and everyone who owns a TV is supposed to pay the license fee. If you don't own a TV, you can opt out, but they don't make it easy. As a visitor watching TV in a hotel or rented accommodation, you do not need a TV license. The owner of the TV pays for the license.

My hotel room only has instant coffee.

Instant coffee is still often the only option in many hotel rooms. As there will be a kettle, you could always buy a travel coffee maker. If you like the hotel, grab yourself a coffee from one of the many local coffee places and mention it to the staff or on a comment card. Also be aware that there may not be a fridge unless you request one in advance.

Mainly for men—If you don't want to be identified as an American abroad:

Leave the tennis shoes, tube socks, shorts and baseball cap at home.

Wear real shoes, full-length trousers (pants) and consider a collared shirt rather than a T-shirt. It might not get you upgraded, but it might save you from being easily targeted as suitable for robbery.

Words and phrases that will identify you as an American:

Referring to Wimbledon as Wimbleton. There is no "t." It's Wimbledon.

On Accident: Whereas an American might do something "on accident," a Brit would do it "by accident."

On Christmas: An American might plan to visit you "on Christmas," but a Brit would come "at Christmas."

York-shire (or any place that ends in "shire"): The sound is "sher," as in Yorksher.

Edinburgh: Sounds like Edinborough. (Don't pronounce it with a "g.")

Write to: They write "to" their MP (Member of Parliament). You write your congressmen without the "to."

Monday/Friday: We prefer "Monday to Friday" rather than "Monday through Friday."

Thank You for Reading

I hope you've had fun learning about the UK and its language and customs. Whether you have been reading because you have a trip planned or because you like British television and want to understand more, I hope that *Put the Kettle On* has answered your questions and also made you laugh.

There is so much to see and do in the UK, and there's some great British TV available. The more we understand each other, the more fun we can have communicating.

I'd love to hear from you if you have anything you think should be added to the next edition.

Acknowledgments

Thanks to the team of British fact checkers who updated me on all that has changed since I moved away. And to my US readers who helped me to clarify information on the American side.

Peter Cusack

Teresa Jack

Bethany Lingard

Jennifer Reeves

About the Author

Trish Taylor was living and working in England, happily settled in her 14-year role as a career counselor and part-time jazz singer. An encounter with a Salsa-dancing American literally swept her off her feet. They married and moved to the United States. She now writes and speaks.

She is the author of a range of self-help books:

Yes! You Are Good Enough: End Imposter Syndrome, Overthinking and Perfectionism and Live the Life YOU Want

Why Am I Scared? Face Your Fears and Learn to Let Them Go

I'm Never Drinking Again: Maybe It's Time to Think About Your Drinking?

A Brief Guide To the Magic of NLP: Neuro-Linguistic Programming for Everyday Life

Co-author of *Respect in the Workplace: You Have to Give It to Get It*

Trish lives in Florida with her husband.

Connect at www.trishtaylorauthor.com.

Made in the USA
Middletown, DE
26 August 2022